Prof. Fuko,

I just wanted to thank you for all the help & friendship you've given me while I've been at Trinity.

I found the following quote which I thought was appropriate for you:

"We must scrupulously guard the civil rights & civil liberties of all our citizens ♡ their background. We must remember that any oppression, any injustice, any hatred is a we... designed to attack our civilization." FDR sai... a greeting to the American Committee for the Protection of foreign-born. I thought of you when I first read it.

I cannot express how important you've been to my Trinity career & how much more pleasant you've made my time here.

Thank you.

Karen von Hardenberg
Class of 1999

Seven Dirty Words and Six Other Stories

SEVEN DIRTY WORDS AND SIX OTHER STORIES

CONTROLLING THE CONTENT OF PRINT AND BROADCAST

Matthew L. Spitzer

Yale University Press
New Haven and London

Designed by James Johnson
and set in Auriga Roman type.
Printed in the United States of America by
Murray Printing Company, Westford, Mass.

Library of Congress Cataloging-in-Publication Data

Spitzer, Matthew Laurence, 1952–
    Seven dirty words and six other stories.

    Includes index.
    1. Censorship—United States.   2. Television—
Censorship—United States.   3. Freedom of speech—
United States.   I. Title.
KF4772.S65   1986   343.73'09946   86–9158
ISBN 0–300–03568–3   347.3039946

*The paper in this book meets the guidelines for
permanence and durability of the Committee on
Production Guidelines for Book Longevity of the
Council on Library Resources.*

10   9   8   7   6   5   4   3   2   1

For Jean Spitzer

A satiric humorist named George Carlin recorded a 12-minute monologue entitled "Filthy Words" before a live audience in a California theater. He began by referring to his thoughts about "the words you couldn't say on the public, ah, airwaves, um, the ones you definitely wouldn't say, ever. . . .

"I have to figure out which ones you couldn't and it came down to seven but the list is open to amendment. . . . The original seven words were, shit, piss, fuck, cunt, cocksucker, motherfucker, and tits. Those are the ones that will curve your spine, grow hair on your hands and (laughter) maybe, even bring us, God help us, peace without honor."

Federal Communications Commission v. Pacifica Foundation, 438 U.S. 726 (1978).

Contents

Preface

This book started when I began to prepare my lectures for Regulation of Broadcasting, the first class I taught as a law professor. The natural place to start, I thought, was with the issue of why broadcasting was a special case. The lectures turned out to be much harder to prepare than I had expected, for each of the arguments in favor of treating broadcasting differently seemed to be weak. Over the ensuing years I taught Regulation of Broadcasting several more times and wrote a couple of articles about broadcasting law, but the increased knowledge I gained did not strengthen the arguments in favor of regulating broadcasting more intrusively than print. Instead, the arguments seemed to lose force. And to make things more troublesome, I became convinced that the differential treatment of broadcasting was not a mere detail in our otherwise satisfactory system of free expression, but was rather the central anomaly.

Faced with this situation I determined to write a law review article that would provide a detailed taxonomy of the various arguments for differential regulation and then appraise their worth. One and a half years later I had produced a manuscript so thick that it could serve as a doorstop, and my colleagues informed me that I had written a short book, rather than an article. Jean Spitzer, my wife, then kindly provided the manuscript with a very extensive edit, sharpening and clarifying the exposition greatly. The *Southern California Law Review* published part of my results first in *Controlling the*

Content of Print and Broadcast, 58 S. Cal. L. Rev. 1349 (1985), but not until the publication of this book have my full thoughts on the matter have been stated.

This book owes much to helpful comments by Robert Bennett, Scott Bice, Richard Craswell, Erwin Chemerinsky, Michael Levine, Roger Noll, Alan Schwartz, Michael Shapiro, Larry Simon, Jean Spitzer, and the participants at the University of Chicago Law and Economics Workshop. Research suggestions from Neil Malamuth and Seymour Feshbach were also very helpful. Lee Ann Duffy, Jim Heller, Steven Jacobi, Ellen Roth, Marc Sherman, Sari Stabler, and Rob Yarin provided research assistance. The financial support of the University of Southern California Faculty Research and Innovation Fund is gratefully acknowledged.

Introduction

WHY does our government regulate the content of broadcast communications more strictly than it regulates the printed word? The principal rationales that have been suggested are: (1) to achieve economic efficiency; (2) to limit socially harmful conduct caused by people's exposure to sexually explicit or violent material; and (3) to prevent children's exposure to a variety of material that may harm them. I hope to show in this book that these rationales cannot support the existing regulatory framework.

The United States now regulates broadcast communications much more intensively than it regulates printed communications. For example, broadcasters must obtain licenses to operate.[1] Federal statutes and regulations require broadcasters to cover fairly all sides of controversial issues of public importance,[2] but printed publications may be biased. Broadcasters must present programming designed to meet the needs and interests of their communities of license,[3] but printed publications need not do so. And a broadcaster must even give free reply time to those whose honesty, character, or integrity has been attacked during the discussion of a controversial issue,[4] whereas a printed publication cannot be required to do so.

This extensive control of broadcast content is embedded within a pervasive system in which the government allocates control of electromagnetic spectrum. Paper, of course, is not allocated but is available to all. The Federal Communications

1

Commission (FCC) directly allocates spectrum between competing uses, such as radio and television broadcasts, electrical power and satellite transmissions, police and fire communications, and even the radio control of model airplanes and boats. Paper, in contrast, is allocated by markets that are free of direct governmental control.

Of course, both market systems and regulatory systems operate against a common background of laws that control content—most importantly the laws of defamation. The laws of defamation deter libelous statements in both print and broadcast, applying the same set of rules to the content of both media. I will not be concerned with these rules. Instead, I will focus on the rules that apply only to the content of one of the media—broadcast.

A brief historical sketch will help to show how idiosyncratic the disparate treatment of print and broadcast really is.[5] When the first amendment to the Constitution—guaranteeing freedom of speech and of the press—was adopted, the print medium was privately owned; individuals held private property rights, enforceable at common law, to paper, ink, and printing presses. According to the original understanding, the first amendment protects this private property system.

Radio communication, in contrast, was not possible until the very end of the nineteenth century. Before World War I, radio communication was used almost exclusively to aid shipping. Then, during the war, the United States Navy commandeered this new technology for military communications. After the war, the Navy sought permanent control of radio, but was rebuffed. Unfortunately, Congress failed to replace the Navy's control of spectrum with an effective system of property rights, and, as radio broadcasting developed during the early 1920s, interference between broadcasters became a serious problem. This was to be expected, because there was no established legal mechanism by which one broadcaster might preclude another from broadcasting on the same frequency. In response, broadcasters attempted to solve the interference problem through voluntary cooperation, but they failed. Herbert Hoover, then secretary of commerce, attempted to create a licensing system, although he had no formal authority to do so. Hoover's efforts failed when the federal courts ruled that he had no discretion to refuse a license to anyone who applied. The ensuing chaos produced intense political pressure for the creation of some rights in electromagnetic spectrum, pressure that culminated in the Federal Radio Act of 1927,[6] which essentially created the regulatory scheme that exists today.

Congress might have chosen to treat spectrum much like paper. It could have established a system of private property in spectrum, creating in effect "deeds" to certain frequencies during certain periods of time and at certain field strengths. Such deeds would have conferred the right to exclude others and would have relied on tort, contract, and criminal laws for enforcement. A person who uses another person's paper may be required to pay for it by means of a tort suit. And someone who steals paper may be criminally liable. An unregulated market in broadcast spectrum would have used tort and criminal law in a similar fashion. Anyone who used someone else's spectrum would have been required to pay for it (and to refrain from using it in the future) by means of a tort suit. And anyone who stole spectrum would have been criminally liable.[7]

This private property approach would have needed no intrusive governmental regulation of broadcast content, and, in effect, would have equalized the treatment of print and broadcast. Instead, Congress created the Federal Radio Commission (later the FCC) to license broadcasters and to regulate broadcast content. This legislative policy choice, later declared constitutional by the Supreme Court, produced the current situation.

Such dramatically different institutional treatment of the media requires more than historical practice to justify it. The question I ask in this book is whether good reasons exist to justify specific forms of such differential treatment. If no such reasons are found, the legitimacy of these differences must be seriously questioned. Also, given the current and probable future receptivity of the federal government to deregulation, exposing the illegitimacy of the regulatory regime may have important practical consequences.

To find such good reasons I will not consider arguments claiming that regulation is, in general, bad, for these arguments cannot distinguish between print and broadcast. Instead, I will examine arguments, each of which contends all of the following: that a difference between the two media exists, that this difference has normative significance, and that some specific form of differential regulation responds directly to the normative distinction.

The first contention concerns the difference, factual or theoretical, between spectrum and paper. For example, if one were to consider the argument that broadcast must be regulated differently from print because children who view crime shows on television tend to become aggressive, then one would have to ask whether children who read crime stories tend to become just as aggressive.

Second, if there is a difference, does it justify treating the two media differently? For example, if one found that children who view crime shows on television tend to become aggressive, but that children who read crime stories do not, one would have identified a difference between the two media. But to justify different treatment of the media one would have to go one step further and believe that producing aggressive children was bad (or good), rather than morally irrelevant.[8]

Third, assuming that a normative difference between the media exists, what specific regulatory treatment does this difference imply? For example, if one found that children who view crime shows on television tend to become aggressive, but that children who read crime stories do not, and if one thought that producing aggressive children was a bad thing, then banning crime shows or limiting the hours in which they are shown might seem wise. However, if the only relevant difference between print and broadcast were this effect on children, then all other special content controls on broadcast, such as the fairness doctrine,[9] would be unjustified.

This analysis rules out the public ownership argument, mentioned rather obliquely by the Supreme Court in *Red Lion Broadcasting Co. v. FCC*,[10] as a good reason for differential regulation. This argument begins by noting that Title 47 of the United States Code declares that the United States, and not its individual citizens, owns the spectrum.[11] The government allows individuals to use the spectrum by giving them licenses, but it need not do so, the argument continues. Therefore, if the government licenses some spectrum to individuals, it can do so subject to conditions, which may include restrictions on content. In contrast, runs the argument, the government does not own paper, and therefore has less freedom to impose content restrictions on print.[12]

The public ownership argument provides no justification for differential content control. First, even if its premise that the government has the power to impose greater content restrictions on broadcasters is correct, this argument shows only that the government *can* impose differential content control, not that it *should* do so. Unless one believes "can implies ought," a belief I completely reject, one must continue to search for a justification—an independent reason for taking action. Second, the public ownership argument's premise that the government has the power to impose differential content control may be wrong. The argument depends on an unsophisticated understanding of the word "own." To say that the government owns some resource is merely a shorthand for describing the various activities the government may lawfully pursue with that resource. The government may own the national park system, but it can neither exclude blacks from the parks nor test atomic weapons there. Private and public rights, justified by independent arguments, may restrict the manner in which the government may use resources that it owns. These observations apply equally well to the spectrum which the government owns. Unless we can find some independent argument for differential content control, the government may not be allowed to impose stricter controls on broadcast.

I will consider rationales related to content as well as those that are more directly concerned with economics. I will analyze the economic rationales because of their historical connection to content rationales. Many have argued that economic efficiency requires a central body to own all of the electromagnetic spectrum (but not paper) and to license it to "trustees." However, according to this argument, because only a very limited number of licenses can be issued, some licensees may gain great power over the marketplace of ideas and our democratic government. To guard against this danger, broadcasters should be subject to content restrictions requiring them to fulfill "fiduciary" obligations to the public by, for example, covering controversial issues in an unbiased fashion.

Rationales that relate directly to content are of two types. First, there is a general argument about television's interaction with and (purported) domination of the human mind. Second, there is a large group of arguments that suggest regulating content because broadcast material tends to incite undesirable behavior. A full treatment of the subject would cover every major argument (that is, the connections between broadcast content and violent acts, voting behavior, and so forth). However, I will deal only with the connections between broadcasting sexual and/or violent matter and sexually aggressive and violent behavior. Not only are these the most commonly mentioned arguments, but the conclusions drawn from the analysis of them will probably apply to the other rationales as well.

I will conclude that none of the surveyed rationales justifies the status quo. In particular, I will find: (1) of the economic rationales, neither traditional scarcity arguments nor industry structure arguments can justify different treatment of the content of the media; (2) the argument about television's domination of the human mind is completely unconvincing; (3) arguments that broadcast erotica is more pernicious than printed erotica are also unconvincing, but existing evidence weakly suggests that broadcasting violent programming may be slightly more harmful than publishing its printed counterpart; and (4) the comparatively easy access children have to television may suggest controlling children's access to broadcast material more strictly than their access to print.

As a consequence, we may wish to zone violent (and, perhaps, sexually explicit) programs into the late hours of the evening. Or we might confine such matter to certain frequencies (channels) and allow only adults to purchase receivers that can decode these signals. *But my analysis suggests that no other differences in the regulatory control of broadcast and print are justifiable.*

I Economic Rationales for Treating the Media Differently

MUCH of the traditional justification for regulating broadcast more extensively than print relies on the following argument: Economic efficiency requires that the government must "own" all the rights to electromagnetic spectrum (but not paper). With this ownership comes the duty to protect the public's right to diverse programming. To guarantee diversity, the government licenses private citizens to broadcast as "trustees" for the public and subjects these trustee broadcasters to content controls to ensure that they fulfill their "fiduciary" obligations.

This argument, dubbed the "fiduciary model," has trationally relied upon the concept of scarcity to show that economic efficiency requires that the government own all the spectrum rights. This fiduciary model has been embraced by the United States Supreme Court, most enthusiastically in Justice Byron White's opinion for a unanimous court in *Red Lion Broadcasting Co. v. FCC.*

There are two basic questions regarding the adequacy of this model. The first is whether economic efficiency truly requires that the government own all broadcast spectrum, but not paper. One may try to forge a connection between economic efficiency and government ownership in several ways. The idea of scarcity traditionally provides the link; only government ownership, it is claimed, can prevent scarcity from destroying economic efficiency in broadcasting. Managerial arguments (that is, only broadcasting needs centralized management to coordinate its many complex technological interactions) and industry structure arguments (that is,

7

unregulated broadcasting, but not print, will tend toward monopoly) might also provide the link. The industry structure arguments are especially important, for they in part sparked the original drive to regulate broadcasting in the 1920s. Thus, these arguments will occupy the bulk of the discussion.

Second, one might ask whether a restriction on the number of broadcasters necessarily implies the control of content. Because I will conclude that there are few justifications for the government to own spectrum, this question is not crucial, and I will treat it only briefly.

1   Property Rights

EACH of the following rationales suggests that paper can be effectively distributed through a market system based on private property rights, but that spectrum cannot. All of the arguments depend, in one way or another, upon the norm of economic efficiency—the value of producing and distributing the mix of goods and services that consumers desire. I do not believe any of these rationales even approaches justifying different regulatory treatment of spectrum.

THE SCARCITY THEORIES[1]

Scarcity rationales have provided the basis for several Supreme Court opinions. In *National Broadcasting Co. v. United States*[2] the majority opinion embraced the scarcity rationale: "Unlike other modes of expression, radio inherently is not available to all. That is its *unique characteristic,* and that is why, unlike other modes of expression, it is subject to governmental regulation."[3] The dissent concurred: "Owing to its physical characteristics radio, unlike the other methods of conveying information, must be regulated and rationed by the government."[4] Twenty-six years later, in *Red Lion Broadcasting Co. v. FCC,*[5] a unanimous Court defended the scarcity rationale against the contention that radio spectrum was not scarce. Plaintiffs argued that technological advances had produced a far more efficient and productive utilization of the radio spectrum than had been possible in 1934. The Court replied that demand for spectrum had grown to the point where not all demand would be satisfied if spectrum were free. When the plaintiffs responded that the existence of allocated but unclaimed UHF television stations demonstrated that spectrum was no longer scarce, the Supreme Court turned aside the challenge; the FCC's allocation of otherwise valuable radio spectrum to a valueless use, the Court claimed, did not prove that the spectrum was not scarce.

Although the scarcity argument was absent from one important Supreme Court decision dealing with broadcasting in 1978,[6] it has continued to be influential.[7] In 1984, the Supreme Court reaffirmed the scarcity theory, albeit in somewhat lukewarm fashion, in *FCC v. League of Women Voters*.[8] The Court squarely based differential treatment of the content of broadcast on the scarcity rationale, and then indicated:

> The prevailing rationale for broadcast regulation based on spectrum scarcity has come under increasing criticism in recent years. Critics, including the incumbent Chairman of the FCC, charge that with the advent of cable and satellite television technology, communities now have access to such a wide variety of stations that the scarcity doctrine is obsolete. *See, e.g.,* Fowler & Brenner, A Marketplace Approach to Broadcast Regulation, 60 Tex. L. Rev. 207, 221–226 (1982). We are not prepared, however, to reconsider our long-standing approach without some signal from Congress or the FCC that technological developments have advanced so far that some revision of the system of broadcast regulation may be required.[9]

There are four versions of the scarcity theory in the cases and legal literature: (1) static technological scarcity; (2) dynamic technological scarcity; (3) excess demand scarcity; and (4) entry scarcity. In addition, this book formulates a fifth version: relative scarcity. Because the United States Supreme Court relies upon the scarcity theory to justify the current regulatory scheme, I must consider all five.

Static Technological Scarcity

This argument notes that everyone cannot broadcast at the same time, in the same place, and on the same frequency without causing intolerable interference. This observation is usually accompanied by a reference to the chaos that existed prior to the passage of the 1927 Radio Act.[10] Paper is different, the defender of spectrum regulation argues, because if two people wish to write different things each can get some paper and write a message, without interfering with the other's. The argument concludes that the only way to deal with broadcast interference is with an FCC invested with broadcast licensing powers. Because such a system of administrative licenses is clearly more economically efficient than a system of no property rights at all (allowing anyone to broadcast on any frequency, at any power, at any time and place), having the FCC is better than not having it.

Static technological scarcity fails to provide a good reason for regulating only electromagnetic spectrum because the two media—print and broadcast—are, as a theoretical matter, *both* scarce. Of course, two broadcasters cannot broadcast at the same time, place, and frequency (and polarization) without causing gibberish. However, the same argument is true of paper: if two people wrote on the same piece of paper both messages might be obscured. Thus, paper is also plagued by static technological scarcity and, as with spectrum, some form of property right (that is, the power to exclude others from the use of the medium) is needed to ensure effective communication.

Is there, perhaps, some fundamental difference between interference on paper and interference on spectrum? If one person were to write on a piece of paper, another would refrain from writing on that paper unless he were to write in the margins, so as to allow both messages to be read. In contrast, might one broadcast even where the result would be loss of all other messages? Such a distinction fails in several respects.

First, people do not *always* write in the margins. If one may visualize walls as very large pieces of paper, overlapping graffiti provide an obvious example of people writing over others' messages in the hope of being seen. Of course, the larger and bolder the second writer is, the more likely the second message is to obliterate the first. In most circumstances, however, writing in the margins is preferable because the second message will be easier to read. But even then, the second message will interfere, in part, with the first. (After all, margins do have a purpose.)

Identical incentives characterize the use of spectrum. First, someone will broadcast directly over another message if he wishes to obliterate the first message in favor of his own. In most cases, however, broadcasting in the marginal bands between other broadcasts will be preferable because the transmission is much easier to receive. But by so doing, the second broadcaster interferes, to some extent, with the original broadcaster's transmission. In sum, there is no fundamental difference here.

Even if one incorrectly concluded that static technological scarcity plagues only spectrum, one would need to regard the regulation of scarce resources as desirable to have a good reason for regulating spectrum. For example, if one believed that scarce goods could not be efficiently produced and distributed through a market system, then economic efficiency might suggest licensing. However, Ronald Coase showed in his 1959 article, *The Federal Communications Commission,* that one can efficiently distribute rights to scarce resources through a market system.[11] Indeed, markets based upon private property rights distribute much that is commonly considered most scarce—diamonds, gold, silver, rare paintings, and so forth. To function, a market needs only a sufficient description of the circumstance in which courts will enforce the owner's power to exclude others. There is nothing inherent in radio spectrum's scarcity that prevents the creation and enforcement of an efficient market in private spectrum rights.[12]

Much work has already been done to develop the parameters of just such a system.[13] One plausible version would involve creating deeds specifying the frequencies, times, and signal intensities for lawful operation. The FCC has in fact implemented a regulatory version of property rights: licenses to broadcast, complete with their rights to the use of some spectrum, are bought and sold frequently. But there is nothing about scarcity or property rights, per se, that requires a regulatory agency—problems can always be handled by private rights and the courts. Because the static technological scarcity argument does not show that regulation will be more economically efficient for spectrum, it does not justify treating paper and spectrum differently.

Dynamic Technological Scarcity

The second version of the scarcity argument claims that while the radio spectrum is inherently limited, one can always produce more newsprint. This argument fails to justify regulating only spectrum for several reasons. First, in a *static* framework, both the amount of paper and the amount of spectrum are limited. At any given time our resources and our ability to use them are quite fixed. This is true of both printing materials (newsprint, presses, and so forth) and broadcast inputs (usable portions of the spectrum, the number of transmitters and receivers, and so forth).

A *dynamic* version of this scarcity theory would claim that one can always grow more trees, but one cannot grow more spectrum. The argument is only half correct—one could indeed produce more newsprint by growing more trees. However, one could also increase research and development in the area of electromagnetic spectrum use, and thus produce a greater "volume" of spectrum in the future. In this way, one can "grow" more spectrum, just as one grows more newsprint.

This basic point sometimes eludes even the most experienced and distinguished commentators. William Van Alstyne, for example, seems to confuse the static and dynamic aspects of scarcity by arguing that, *with a given technology,* one can have only a certain number (500) of broadcast stations in a locality, but one can always bring more paper into a locality. He is wrong. At some point one will have brought all available paper (in the short run) to a locality. From that point forward, one must invest in the technology of producing and transporting paper to increase the amount of paper, much as one must invest in technology to increase the usable spectrum.

Further, the spectrum's potential is currently quite unlimited, for we have yet to develop the higher frequencies of transmission. In a closely related context, the recent development of fiber optic cable transmissions represents a small break-through in the use of visible light (which uses extremely high frequencies) for communication. In sum, the dynamic technological scarcity rationale cannot distinguish between paper and spectrum.

Excess Demand Scarcity

This rationale asserts that spectrum is different from paper in that there are more people who wish to have spectrum rights, particularly VHF television licenses, than there are rights to distribute. In contrast, there is no such excess demand for paper.

Although this observation is correct in itself, it proves nothing. More people want VHF television licenses than can be satisfied because these valuable licenses are given away without charge. If one charges nothing for the rights to a valuable resource, then anyone who values it at all will want it. In such circumstances, demand will always exceed supply. In particular, if one were to charge nothing for paper, demand for paper would certainly exceed supply, and excess demand scarcity would characterize paper, just as it does spectrum. There is no excess demand for paper at present because its price is determined by an unregulated market.

Entry Scarcity

The entry scarcity argument claims that anyone can buy some paper and a small printing press, but, because of licensing, not everyone can start a radio station. At Senator Robert Packwood's hearings on the treatment of the first amendment in broadcasting, he and Thomas Krattenmaker agreed that this argument is wrong because it depends on the comparison of incomparable things.[14] They argued that, if one equates a tiny printing press to a citizen's band radio transmission, as one should, then would-be broadcasters can go out and start a little radio station. Although they were right to reject this version of the scarcity argument as a method of distinguishing spectrum and paper, they did so for the wrong reason. If the FCC were to allocate no spectrum for citizens' uses, then no one could "just start" a little radio station. However, the entry scarcity argument would still be wrong because the current differences in ease of entry are products of, not justifications for, different treatment of the media. To make a useful comparison, one must ask if, *given similar legal and institutional treatment,* there would still be a difference between accessibility to print and broadcast. Such a difference seems quite unlikely, particularly given the similarities in the economics of the two media discussed in chapter 2.

This same criticism also negates any attempt to counter the entry scarcity argument by first arguing that entry is needed only to ensure a robust marketplace of ideas, and then demonstrating that there are many more broadcasters than newspapers.[15] Such arguments lose their force because the existing relative *number* of broadcasters and print publishers is a product of current institutional treatment of the two media, and therefore has little inherent significance.

If we could equalize the legal and institutional treament of the two media, then we could appraise the entry scarcity rationale by asking whether there were different barriers to entry for print and broadcast. Such different barriers could originate only in the differing economics of communicating through the two media. In chapter 2, I will search for those economic differences.

Relative Scarcity

The relative scarcity argument concedes that both paper and broadcast spectrum are scarce, but maintains that spectrum is substantially *more* scarce. What might this mean? The simplest approach might be to count "units" of broadcast spectrum and pieces of paper. However, there can be no units without first defining the communications job for which the medium is to be used. To see this, consider the following two jobs: (1) a parent communicating to a child in a different room of the same house and (2) ground control communicating to an astronaut in geostationary orbit. Assume that the family members own cheap, sloppy radio transmitters and receivers that require a very wide band of spectrum to operate, but have good eyesight and can pass written messages to one another. Also assume that the astronaut has very sensitive radio gear, but only average eyesight. In the parent-to-child scenario, the minimal band of spectrum needed for communication on the sloppy and insensitive radios (in other words, a unit of spectrum) will be quite large, but the unit of paper needed for the same message will be very small. In the ground control-to-astronaut situation, things are reversed. The minimal band of spectrum needed to communicate with the astronaut's sensitive radio receiver (the unit of spectrum) will be very small, whereas the smallest piece of paper required to send the same message must be quite large to be visible from 23,600 miles above the earth.

These two examples prove that units depend on job definitions, and that depending on the job, either spectrum or paper may be more scarce. Sometimes, as in the first situation, spectrum is scarcer than paper, but other times, as in the second situation, the reverse is true. These examples also emphasize that neither paper nor spectrum, by themselves, communicate anything. Both media are part of a communication *system*. Paper requires machinery that can place the message upon the paper (a pen or printing press) and a means of transporting the paper from writer to reader (a truck, plane). Spectrum requires both transmitters and receivers. The nature of the communications system, for both paper and spectrum, changes in response to the job.

Even after we view paper and spectrum in this fashion, the relative scarcity argument gains no strength. In many instances, only one medium will be suitable for a particular job. What paper system, for example, compares to the broadcast of music? Obviously, none. Yet another problem for the comparison of systems is that, for some purposes, paper systems are more scarce (ground to astronaut), while for others (room to room) clearly the opposite is true. Consequently, we cannot conclude that in general either print or broadcast is inherently scarcer.

At this point, one might object that the counting methodology seems fairly unsophisticated and that we should focus instead upon the costs of print and broadcast to determine relative scarcity. Would this approach prove any more effective than counting? No, and for exactly the same reasons that derailed the attempt to count. Just as there are no units of spectrum or paper until one first defines the communication job, depending on this definition either spectrum or paper will cost more. Hence, this cost-related version of the relative scarcity argument also fails to distinguish between paper and spectrum.

The Last Scarcity Argument

In *A Marketplace Approach to Broadcast Regulation*[16] FCC Chairman Mark Fowler and coauthor Daniel Brenner reject scarcity justifications for regulating only broadcast. First, they correctly note that "virtually all goods in society are scarce," but then reverse their field and try to show that "other factors should lead to a rejection of the belief that a condition of true scarcity prevails in broadcasting." Their arguments include: (1) we can add channels if we are willing to tolerate increased interference; (2) advertising dollars "restrict broadcast opportunities more than does the number of channels"; (3) the FCC's table of allocations has structured the broadcasting industry; (4) some UHF TV licenses go unclaimed; (5) one can purchase a VHF license; and (6) there are substitute entertainment forms for over-the-air broadcast.

Only if we read "true scarcity" to mean an uncommon form of scarcity might these arguments support Fowler and Brenner's point. Unfortunately, Fowler and Brenner do not explicitly define true scarcity, so we cannot be certain of the exact relationship of these six arguments to their conclusion. Probably they are implicitly referring to relative scarcity, which I have already discussed. If so, they are correct—spectrum is not relatively more scarce than paper. If Fowler and Brenner have something else in mind, their argument is a complete mystery.

In sum, none of these basic scarcity arguments—static,

dynamic, excess demand, entry, and relative scarcity—provides a relevant difference between print and broadcast. Thus, none provides a justification for treating them differently. It follows accordingly that none of these rationales supports regulating the content of broadcast transmissions more strictly than the content of printed communications.

MANAGEMENT RATIONALES

Another set of arguments also focuses on interference. These arguments acknowledge that interference affects both spectrum and paper, but maintain that only radio interference produces an economically inefficient allocation of the medium. They do not suggest that, once particular *uses* have been chosen for particular blocks of spectrum, a market cannot select *users*. Indeed, radio and television broadcast licenses, representing the rights to use particular blocks of spectrum, are transferred between users virtually every day. Therefore, the discussions below apply only to the issue of whether or not a market can choose efficiently between competing uses—for example, between having one television station or many radio stations on the same frequency bandwidth.

Capital Markets and Management Failures

Nicholas Johnson, a former commissioner of the FCC, has argued that a market allocation of spectrum will fail either because modern business managers fail to maximize profit—leading to inefficient use of resources—or because imperfections in capital markets prevent those with superior ideas and abilities from gaining control of resources. Administrative allocation, he argues, complete with the attendant restrictions on content, is a better alternative.[17] Whether or not Johnson is right about modern business managers and capital markets, he provides no justification for treating print and broadcast differently, unless his arguments apply only to one of the media, and not the other. However, modern print publishers and broadcasters go to the same sources for capital and hire the same types of managers. In fact, many broadcasters, magazines, and newspapers are owned by media conglomerates. Therefore, Johnson's arguments are equally applicable to both media.

Complexity

The simplest management rationale asserts that minimizing electromagnetic interference economically is too complex a job for the market to handle satisfactorily. In this vein, Glen Robinson argues that a market allocation of spectrum would probably lead to inefficient recombinations of frequencies that would ignore the interests of many spectrum users (for example, their investments in receivers and other equipment).[18]

Such an argument, based on complexity alone, cannot stand. Allocating paper is just as complicated a task as allocating spectrum. After all, the American paper industry produces notebook paper, paper currency, brown paper bags, paper plates, paper kites, toilet paper, facial tissues, cardboard boxes, cigarette rolling papers, greeting cards, gift-wrapping paper, milk cartons, and, of course, newsprint. One could easily ask questions about paper like those Robinson asks about spectrum. What, for example, prevents the paper industry from destroying this country's huge investment in cheap pens by producing only very soft and absorbent writing paper? Similarly, why does the paper industry not endanger the health and comfort of infants by producing wax paper diapers? The market mechanism responds to such concerns for both paper and spectrum; individuals shape demand by protecting their own health, comfort, and previous investments, and entrepreneurs, hoping to reap rewards, try to respond to the individuals' demands. The complexity of the industry does not, in itself, explain the market's inability to allocate spectrum. Rather, to complete this argument, one must explain why a market can work for paper but not for spectrum. In the following section, I will investigate two possible reasons, both based on externalities.

Large Numbers of Parties

The basic story. Interference between spectrum users often involves many parties. Also, changes in demand and technology may create opportunities to recombine large bands of spectrum for valuable new uses. But if the numerous parties involved try to contract with one another to produce more valuable arrangements, strategic behavior (holding out or free riding) may defeat their efforts. As a result, a private market might produce an inflexible system, incapable of responding efficiently to changes in demand and technology. As the analysis below will show, this probably is a genuine difference between spectrum and paper. It is unclear, however, whether this difference justifies regulating broadcast because numerous responses, less severe than regulation, are available.

To understand the problem, consider the strategic complications produced by the need to segregate different types of radio emissions. By way of background, there are various types of radio emissions: pulse, continuous-wave, high-power, low-power, and so forth. All radio signals tend to interfere not only with other signals on their own transmission frequencies, but with other, usually adjacent, ones as well.[19] Moreover, certain kinds of signals often cause greater interference in some applications than in others. By segregating usages accordingly, therefore, one can increase the efficiency of spectrum use. For example, one may be able to increase the efficiency of a spectrum band by limiting it to only low-power, continuous-wave transmissions.

How might the existence of large numbers of parties in the market prevent the efficient recombination of spectrum rights? Where only two parties are involved, the market can be expected to do the job efficiently enough. Consider the following scenario: B is transmitting a continuous-wave (CW) signal at X Hertz. A is transmitting a pulsed signal on an adjacent frequency, but his signal is causing $1,000,000 worth of interference to B's. A's pulsed signal would cause no interference to a *pulsed* signal at B's frequency, however, and CW signals interfere with neither pulsed nor CW signals. The value of B's

CW signal, without interference, is $1,500,000; the value of A's pulsed signal is $350,000; A's frequency, on CW, is worth $250,000.

Case 1: A has the legal right to interfere with B's signal. B will pay A somewhere between $100,000 and $1,000,000 to convert to a CW signal.

Case 2: A has no right to interfere with B's signal. A will voluntarily convert to a CW signal, for he can offer $100,000 at most to B for permission to interfere, but B would not accept less than $1,000,000.

In both cases A will convert to CW because adjacent CW frequencies are worth $1,750,000, while neighboring pulse and CW signals are worth only $850,000. As long as bargaining can proceed smoothly, broadcasters should be able to efficiently segregate spectrum by use.

Increasing the number of players, so that now A_1 through A_{10} are interfering with B_1 through B_{10}, may make it much more costly and difficult for the market to function. In a situation like case 1, where the A's have a legal right to interfere with the B's signals, it may be difficult for the B's to secure agreements from *all* of the A's to switch; each A may hold out for a greater share of the wealth than is proportionally created by the switch. Also, there may be free rider problems among the B's. Each B, hoping that the other B's will pay the A's enough without him, might refuse to contribute toward paying the A's to switch. If each B adopts this strategy, no one will pay. Strategic problems like these might prevent the market from segregating types of use and, more generally, impede any value-increasing recombinations of spectrum rights. An administrative agency might do better.

There is also the question of whether disputes between many parties might produce litigation costs that exceed the cost of running an administrative agency. Two factors suggest that there may be little basis for choice between courts and administration. First, there are many horror stories involving exhorbitant lawyers' fees and lengthy delays in both courts and administrative agencies, suggesting that both fora may be terribly costly. Second, many of the institutional features that shape the costs of fact-finding and delay in court and administrative agency decisions are under the control of the enforcing body. For example, when courts must find facts in extremely large, complex cases, they often resort to techniques that resemble an administrative agency's, such as appointing masters. Therefore, to answer the question of enforcement costs, one would need a theory that predicts a court's behavior in such cases, and also litigants' reactions to it. This task is beyond the scope of this book. However, nothing strongly suggests either that courts or litigants would behave substantially differently when litigating over spectrum rights than they do in other multiparty civil litigation or that courts would be likely to be much more expensive for enforcing spectrum rights than are administrative agencies. Consequently, until someone offers convincing data or theoretical arguments on this issue, I will put aside enforcement costs as a rationale for administrative allocation of spectrum rights.

The issue, then, is essentially an empirical one: will a market in spectrum rights be more or less efficient at reconstituting and recombining rights, as conditions dictate, than an administrative agency? Unfortunately, as there are no dispositive data to rely upon, any answer must be considered speculative.

The following discussion will make analogies to land use to explore possible private and public institutional responses, short of complete administrative control of spectrum rights, to the problem of inflexibility. Some governmental regulation in the form of zoning or eminent domain power, probably on behalf of private parties, might help to alleviate the problem. Neither form of regulation, however, would justify control of broadcast content.

Some institutional responses.   Both the market and the government could provide institutions to cope with externalities and allow for flexible recombinations of spectrum rights. With regard to mixing *types* of use, the problems of spectrum allocation resemble those of land use; many people believe that intermixing heavy industrial, light industrial, commercial and residential land uses produces external diseconomies. These diseconomies, of course, involve many people. Consequently, strategic behavior might impede the market's segregation of different uses. Most areas in the United States have employed some form of zoning to deal with the attendant problems.

Some of these problems, however, may require no governmental solution after all. Covenants, easements, and rules of homeowner association regulations may be effective enough in dealing with strategic behavior. To illustrate, until recently Houston, Texas, had no zoning regulations whatsoever, satisfactorily relying instead on such alternative mechanisms. This approach could be applied to spectrum as well. Covenants, easements, and spectrum users associations could be created for the radio spectrum, with brokers and developers taking a large role in radio allocation, much as they now do in land.

Zoning regulations tend to focus on general classes of use, prohibiting intermixture of characteristics that destroy value, for example, residential and commercial. They do not, usually, stop clothing stores and camping equipment stores from operating in the same area, for these uses are compatible. Such an approach, if applied to spectrum, would restrict portions of the airwaves to uses that do not cause costly interference. One might, for example, set aside portions of the spectrum for pulsed transmissions and others for continuous-wave, but one would not initially zone some of the spectrum for radio broadcasting and some for other industrial uses, such as microwave relays. Of course, this approach would require sensitive planning. The planner would first have to determine which portions of the spectrum are innately suited to particular types of transmission. (This task is not unlike that of land zoners who must anticipate which of a city's areas will be most suitable for residences and which will be more valuable as commercial areas.)

Even with the best of intentions, however, spectrum planners could err, destroying wealth instead of creating it and forcing users to operate on inappropriate frequencies. If we assume that telecommunications will continue to enjoy rapid technological development and that bureaucratic planners would be slow to modify zone assignments—two quite plausible assumptions—then the zones would always be wrong. Therefore, one should not embrace a spectrum zoning plan too readily.[20]

Where changing demand or technology calls for recombining and reallocating many spectrum rights to create value, the market may need assistance. There may be situations in which perhaps a hundred or more parties are involved. For example, switching from small, terrestrial broadcasts to Direct Broadcast Satellite (DBS) transmissions[21] may require a DBS operator to buy out many terrestrial users to avoid signal interference. As the number of terrestrial users increases, so does the chance of bargaining breakdown. Some potential DBS broadcasters might fail to reach an agreement with terrestrial hold-outs and never broadcast.

One would expect the would-be DBS operator to avoid some hold-out problems by employing agents to purchase the needed spectrum rights. These agents would acquire and amalgamate spectrum rights in the same way that agents for land purchasers acquire and consolidate blocks of land for large-scale development. As a result, the market itself might handle hold-out problems, at least when recombinations of spectrum rights look attractive enough to invite this process. But again, as the number of parties grows very large, such a solution becomes increasingly unlikely.

In land use, the government copes with such problems by employing the power of eminent domain, forcing small, private landholders to sell to a single purchaser. The single purchaser may be public (the government itself), as in the case of highway construction, or private, as in the case of urban renewal projects.[22] The government could conceivably use eminent domain to recombine spectrum rights and thereby eliminate hold-out problems. Such a taking of spectrum rights would promote efficient spectrum utilization in the presence of a market failure and would almost certainly be a "public use" as required by the fifth amendment.[23] Nothing in the complexity rationale suggests that the government must ultimately hold title to the frequencies. Therefore, the power of eminent domain need be exercised only on behalf of private parties.*

Before the power of eminent domain can be exercised, some practical questions will need attention. One would need to determine which private party can invoke eminent domain, under what circumstances, and how much he must pay to each small right-holder. These problems are identical to those encountered in the land-use situation. Whoever would invoke eminent domain power would doubtless be required to pay the small right-holder at least some facsimile of "fair market value." To insure that only value-increasing transfers occur, we might also include a 10 or 20 percent bonus compensation. Some sort of self-selection system, in which the offeror steps forward to register a bid, might be established. This process would have a private party come forward, state his intention to amalgamate a set of rights, guarantee the funds necessary to compensate the other parties, and then await a judicial (or administrative) determination of the appropriate compensation. Other, more specific, administrative rules could make sure the system operates reasonably smoothly.

A similar argument focuses on the federal government's need to negotiate treaties with foreign governments regarding transborder flows of radio waves. If a reassignment or recombination of various blocks of spectrum seems necessary for a treaty, it might be cheaper and easier for the government to negotiate if it "owned" the spectrum rights.

This argument depends on some empirical assumptions about the ease of using eminent domain to recombine spectrum, as opposed to reassigning licenses. Under the current system, when the government tries to reassign licenses, it

---

*There should be no great concern about the communication interests of those required to sell their spectrum rights. Upon receiving the compensation money, these people should be able to buy another set of spectrum rights. If the evolving market structure were to make this impossible for spectrum alone, and not for print, then one would have a serious difference to worry about. However, as the following analysis will show, the market structures should be quite similar for print and broadcast, suggesting that this concern should apply equally well (or poorly) to both media.

inevitably must hold hearings and deal with political pressure from reassigned broadcasters and court challenges to the attempted action. There is no clear reason why an eminent domain procedure should be more difficult.

Finally, then, complexity seems to justify the use of both zoning and eminent domain for broadcast, but neither is needed for print. However, there is no obvious connection between either zoning or eminent domain and differential control of content, the main focus of this book. The likely need for zoning and eminent domain, therefore, cannot justify content control.

The discussion above presumes, quite reasonably, that the details of an eminent domain scheme can be worked out satisfactorily. If this is wrong, then there are two other possible justifications that I must briefly note. One contends that the fact of governmental ownership alone suggests the need for differential control of content.[24] The second concedes that if the government were to allocate and license the spectrum (to which it held title) so as to produce virtually identical market structure in broadcast and print, then there would be little justification for differential content control. However, it continues, if the government were to allocate spectrum so as to greatly concentrate broadcast vis-à-vis print, protecting freedom of expression might require different controls on content in the two media. However, until someone produces convincing data or theories showing that eminent domain cannot be used for spectrum, and I doubt that anyone can, these two justifications for differential content control need not be faced.

Public parks. Administrative control of spectrum rights might be needed should we want to create "electromagnetic parks"—public commons where individuals can "meet" at random, play, and speak with one another. The reference here, of course, is to the current citizens' band. The unassisted market might fail to provide such public spectrum "parks" much as it fails to provide land parks in urban environments. Again the problem is one of externalities. A park benefits people from whom it is too difficult to extract payment. As a result, no profit maximizing private party has the incentive to provide one. Instead, the government must step in, provide the parks, and remedy the market failure. No similar problem seems to exist in the print medium.

This problem of public goods, like that of hold-outs, can easily be remedied through the use of eminent domain. Just as states and cities condemn private landholdings to secure parkland, so could they condemn spectrum rights to form a citizens' band. Should the citizens' band ever be unwanted, the rights could be sold back to private parties, just as is sometimes done with public parkland. Nothing about this characteristic of the broadcast market dictates that an administrative body must hold all title to spectrum, make allocative decisions, or control content.

Only two concerns will likely justify regulatory intervention into the spectrum market. One is the need for public "parks." The other is the need to recombine spectrum allocations in response to changes in demand and technology.[25] Zoning approaches and use of eminent domain should overcome such difficulties. However, neither the creation of public parks nor the use of zoning and eminent domain provides any justification for governmental control of content. Just because we may have some need for the government to sponsor a public park in broadcasting—the citizens' band—implies nothing about any governmental role in controlling what may be said in the park. Similarly, the use of zoning or eminent domain to recombine portions of the spectrum, for example, from many FM radio stations into one television station, gives the government no reason at all to control the content of what is broadcast over those frequencies. Because both creation of public parks and the use of zoning and eminent domain are irrelevant to controlling content, neither can be used to justify differential control of content in print and broadcast.

2 Industry Structure and Monopoly

T HE industry structure rationale for regulating spectrum, but not paper, first assumes that zoning and eminent domain can satisfactorily deal with spectrum management problems, but maintains that some fundamental difference between the media justifies regulating only spectrum. This difference, continues the argument, would produce a monopoly or oligopoly of the airwaves, thereby abrogating[1] *all* first amendment and economic efficiency values. To prevent such a monopoly, goes the argument, the government must create a regulatory agency that can curb the power of broadcasting firms.

To appraise this rationale, I will first briefly compare the economics of broadcast in the absence of regulation to the economics of print and then ask if differences between the two justify differential content control.

PRINT

Newspaper Supply

Printed publications are produced in three stages: creating, editing, and transmitting.[2] Except, perhaps, in the formulation of national news, printing produces no significant economies of scale in the first stages of production. In large city daily newspapers, reporters, news services, editorial writers, and columnists write the nonadvertising content. Virtually anyone can assemble, on a small scale at least, these factors of production. In brief, "neither creation nor editing requires much capital investment."[3] In contrast, the transmission phase of printing and delivering the paper produces substantial economies of scale. These economies have four main sources.

To start, there are "first copy costs." As the second copy of the newspaper is identical to the first, no additional costs are incurred writing or editing it.[4] Of course, one might spend more on the first two stages to attract more readers and thus *sell* more copies. However, for any fixed set of content, as the number of readers increases, the average cost per reader of creating and editing the paper declines.

Second, printing and distributing the paper produce their own economies of scale.[5] In general, over very wide ranges of production, it costs less to print and distribute the $n+1st$ copy of a newspaper than it does each of the first n copies. Once a printing plant is ready to print an issue, one need only feed a few more sheets of newsprint into the press to get another copy. One can deliver this additional paper at low marginal cost by using the already established delivery system (for example, the bag on the carrier's bicycle). However, delivery costs will eventually climb as delivery routes spread out from the city into sparsely populated regions.

Third, there are declining marginal costs in "bundling." It costs less to increase the paper's size from $n+2$ pages to $n+4$ than it does to go from n pages to $n+2$. Hence, it is less expensive to produce one "fat" paper than two papers half its size. As Bruce Owen notes, "this means that 'general' newspapers can drive 'specialized' newspapers out of business, by incorporating the specialized content and specialized advertising as a supplemental part of the paper."[6]

Finally, the commercial value of advertising space increases with circulation, thereby producing another economy of scale.

Newspaper Demand

Newspapers sell their readers news, entertainment, editorial commentary, and consumer information.[7] To advertisers, newspapers sell an "audience." Reader and advertiser demand are interrelated: demand for advertising space increases with a newspaper's readership.[8] Similarly, reader demand grows with the number of ads the newspaper contains. As a paper becomes very large, however, and begins to serve a larger area, these cross effects diminish. Readers and advertisers who are located far from one another care little about reaching each other. This diminishing advertiser and reader demand serves to limit the area in which a profit-maximizing daily will operate.[9] Reader demand for local news does the same thing, as news of highly local interest has little value for readers outside that locality. At some point, further bundling of local news will no longer be worth the added cost. The newspaper can try to overcome this problem with regional editions, but only at the expense of some of the scale economies in transmission.[10]

Newspaper Industry Structure

The limits of scale economies of production and demand combine to allow smaller publications to compete with large daily newspapers.[11] First, smaller newspapers in "satellite" cities provide local news and advertising, while the larger, major newspapers provide national and regional news, as well as advertising for regional businesses (for example, chain stores and franchises).

Second, the market has room for increasingly specialized publications. Neighborhood papers can compete successfully with the satellite and major regional papers. The neighborhood papers commonly derive all of their revenue from advertising on behalf of local merchants and are often distributed on a weekly, rather than a daily basis. Still other publications, like foreign-language newspapers, political fringe papers, and alternative lifestyle publications, cater to special interests, rather than geographically-based readerships.[12]

Altogether, these various publications form an umbrella industry structure.[13] The regional papers are at the top, with the satellites on a second level, and several neighborhood papers below each satellite. The special interest publications may show up on two levels at once.

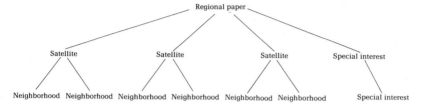

Recently, *USA Today* joined the *Wall Street Journal* as a national publication. Although these papers have yet to achieve the sort of market penetration enjoyed by the regionals (compare the 1,332,974 average daily national circulation of *USA Today*,[14] with the 1,064,392 regional circulation of the *Los Angeles Times*,[15]) they may be regarded as the highest level of the umbrella structure if the reader so desires. None of the following analysis is thereby changed.

Regional newspapers also face competition from national newsmagazines, which also offer national and regional news and advertising. These publications, as well as the UPI and AP news services, enjoy significant economies of scale in the gathering and editing of national news. Broadcast is another strong competitor at the regional level, for through it advertisers can economically reach more diffuse audiences than they could with print.[16]

Supply and Demand of Periodicals

Periodicals and newspapers face, with a few exceptions, very similar kinds of production costs and demand constraints regarding both news and advertising.[17] One exception is that timeliness, in both news and advertising, is less important for periodicals than it is for newspapers. Even newsmagazines such as *Newsweek* or *Time* do not labor under the short deadline pressures confronting daily newspapers, allowing a greater scheduling flexibility. This flexibility allows periodicals to share presses with one another. A second exception is that periodicals, unlike newspapers, mainly respond to demand for subject matter unrelated to geography. The last and most important exception is that periodicals are delivered by a public utility, the United States Postal Service. This circumstance has prevented vertical integration in the transmission phase of periodicals, and has allowed many competing firms to produce periodicals and then transmit them through the Postal Service.

Newspaper and Periodical Market Structure

Major newspapers and periodicals have dramatically different market structures. The newspapers own all facets of their operation, from production of content through the transmission phase, which is a natural monopoly. Such vertical integration may increase efficiency; much of what a daily paper prints is, as mentioned above, highly timely, and integration of the three phases may speed up production, thereby saving some of the value of the paper's contents.[18] Vertical integration may also represent the attempt of the owner of the transmission phase to exploit his monopoly power.[19] Whatever the reason for integration, few major American cities have more than one daily newspaper.[20] Although one could imagine an industry composed of many independent reporters and editors, perhaps organized into small reporting and editing firms, competing with one another and then contracting with transmission phase operators to publish their product, such a structure cannot be found.

In contrast, consumers can purchase many competing periodicals. The three stages of production tend to be unintegrated in periodical publication. The United States Postal Service's status as common carrier has been largely responsible for this.[21] As a consequence, the industry structure allows freelance writers to compose work to sell to periodicals (stage 1), which edit the pieces (stage 2), and then arrange for printers to print and distribute the finished copies (stage 3).

BROADCASTING

Supply and Demand

How do the economics of commercial television compare to those of print? Broadcast and print both use the same three stages of production: creation, editing, and transmission. In both media only transmission and national news production generate significant scale economies. Most of television's entertainment, however, is created in a process unique to that medium. Independent producers procure scripts, from either freelance or staff writers, and then videotape dramatic performances of the scripts.[22] These programs are usually distributed through the major networks (CBS, NBC, or ABC) and transmitted to viewers by local stations. Unaffiliated (non-network) stations purchase entertainment programming directly from syndicates or program packagers.[23] In sum, there is very little vertical integration in this entertainment programming system.

Television news, however, is almost always produced by a vertically integrated unit. Reporters, editors, and producers almost all work for the licensees, either directly in local news production or indirectly on national network programs. An exception is Turner's Cable News Network, which is shown over CATV systems that are not owned by Turner's enterprises. Instead, there are long-term, stable contractual arrangements between Turner and the media that may be viewed as a type of vertical integration. This integration in news operations reflects the need for fast and dependable functioning to conserve the value of timely material. Unaffiliated stations can purchase news from independent producers, like the Cable News Network.

The networks help local stations realize economies of scale in the transmission phase by brokering between both program producers and national advertisers, on the one hand, and local affiliated broadcasters, on the other. "First copy costs" produce substantial economies for broadcasters just as they do for print publishers; once the show has been created, it costs nothing extra, in terms of production, to show it to ten million viewers rather than to just one.

The actual broadcasting itself also generates economies of scale. To increase the effective range of a terrestrial (as opposed to satellite) television station's signal, one either increases the signal's power or adds a second transmission facility. We will assume that over a very wide geographic range, it is cheaper to increase signal power than to build another transmission facility. This assumption is perfectly true only for an infinite plane with a continuously distributed population. In fact, clustered population centers, the curvature of the earth, the existence of mountains, hills, buildings, and the line-of-sight characteristics of FM transmissions all complicate the picture substantially. It may be cheaper, in some circumstances, to erect an additional low-power transmitter in a small community than to increase the power of a distant transmitter.[24] Such complications will not be worked into my analysis for at least two reasons: (1) interconnection of terrestrial transmitters into networks can generate economies of scale similar to those theoretically achievable by a single large, powerful transmitter; and (2) the assumption of large economies of scale produces the strongest possible case based upon market structure for treating broadcast transmissions more restrictively than printed ones.

Direct broadcast satellite (DBS) transmitters provide an even more efficient means of covering very large areas and may soon render their terrestrial counterparts obsolete. A DBS transmitter can broadcast directly to home receivers from satellites in geostationary orbit at 23,600 miles above the earth. The area of reception, termed a "footprint," can span an entire time zone and can stretch from northern Mexico to Canada. Further, because DBS transmissions "rain" out of the sky, they can arrive at the viewers' antennae relatively free of the interference commonly caused by objects such as mountains or tall buildings. Hence, considering cost per viewer, the cheapest transmission process may now reach many tens of millions of viewers. For the purposes of the following discussion, DBS will be treated as the transmission method for the largest areas. The discussion would not be altered significantly, however, if it concentrated instead upon high-powered terrestrial transmitters.

The existing industry structure, which includes only three major over-the-air networks, represents the adaptation of firms to the constraints of regulation. These constraints may have slowed the introduction of DBS technology and may have restricted the possible number of commercial television broadcasters. They have certainly prevented existing television broadcasters from increasing the power of their transmitters. The FCC's allocation, in a table of assignments of VHF and UHF television licenses, creates a moderate number of small, relatively low-power television stations. As a practical matter, technical interference between signals on the same frequency limits the number of local stations. To avoid significantly degrading each other's signals, two transmitters broadcasting simultaneously on the same frequency must broadcast at a power level so low that there will be an area between them where neither transmitter's signal can be received. Thus, the more local television stations there are, the more unserved areas one can expect to find. The FCC, spurred by intense congressional interest, has increased the number of local community television outlets, correspondingly reducing the number of good quality TV signals for most viewers. In fact, under the FCC's table of license assignments, many major communities have only three good signals, and substantial areas of the nation receive no good quality over-the-air signal at all.

The current table of assignments, with its emphasis on local stations, accommodates only three commercial television networks. A fourth network would be at a great competitive disadvantage, for it would be required either to forgo broadcasting or to broadcast with an inferior signal in many major markets. If the FCC were to revise the table of assignments, reducing the number of communities with local signals and increasing to four the number of good quality signals most viewers could receive, a fourth network could probably survive.[25]

DBS, which will be able to broadcast between thirty and forty television channels nationwide in the foreseeable future,[26] could drastically change this market structure. Satellites could transmit signals that virtually everyone would be able to receive. In addition, DBS may also provide "bundling" economies of *scope,* similar to those found in newspapers. (Recall that an industry has economies of scope if it is cheaper for one firm to produce a set of products than it is for several firms to produce one product each.) It may be much cheaper to utilize one satellite that can broadcast fifteen signals than to use fifteen separate satellites, each capable of transmitting only one signal. In this way, a firm owning a fifteen-channel satellite may have lower costs than a firm that attempts to operate with several single-channel satellites. These bundling economies of scope may provide a difference between the economics of satellite and the economics of terrestrial broadcast.

Hypothetical Market Structure of Broadcasting with Property Rights in Spectrum

What would happen to the structure of television broadcasting if electromagnetic spectrum were sold in private markets similar to those for paper? Although the inquiry is highly speculative, a few educated guesses are possible. For one thing, television would be transmitted regionally over DBS.[27] Much would depend upon the status of the satellite transmitters. If private corporations owned and operated the satellites without restraint, they might vertically integrate the transmission phase into the creation and editing phases. The integration would most likely occur in news programming, but could occur in entertainment as well. If, on the other hand, satellites were treated as public utilities, and producers were guaranteed non-discriminatory access to the means of transmission, the industry would become more competitive (actually monopolistically competitive) in the creation and editing phases, resembling, in that respect, the periodical and book publishing industries. Of course, if the economies of "bundling" channels are small in DBS transmissions (compared to the level of demand in the market) or if there is substantial intermodal (DBS, CATV, terrestrial broadcast) substitutability, or if all broadcast is via terrestrial transmitters, which lack bundling economies of scope, then no regulation of transmission as a common carrier would be indicated for broadcast, although it still might make sense for high-speed printing plants used for daily newspapers.[28] In any event, independent writers and producers could sell their products to independent programmers, who, in turn, would broadcast them via transmission capacity rented on the public utility satellite.

Most terrestrial television broadcasters probably would not survive. Perhaps each large metropolitan area could support one or two such stations, which would operate on frequencies like VHF, which are ill suited to satellite broadcast. They would supply local news, weather, sports, and advertisements and might operate only during the morning and early evening hours, assuming demand for local news and programming would be greatest then. These local broadcasters would most likely share frequencies with industrial or business users, whose demand would be greatest during weekday working hours. During the rest of the day the terrestrial broadcasters' frequencies could be used for other things, perhaps for business purposes or maybe additional DBS signals. Of course, cable television, although serving much smaller geographic areas than the regional broadcasters, would, where available, provide effective competition for regional broadcasters.

Together, DBS transmitters, regional terrestrial broadcasters, and cable would create an umbrella industry structure much like that found along geographic lines in newspapers and along subject matter lines in periodicals.

What would happen to "free" (advertiser-sponsored) television if spectrum were bought and sold in an unregulated market? Some free television would almost certainly survive, although probably not as much as exists today in major metropolitan areas. A simple example demonstrates why. Assume that there are thirty million television homes in a satellite transmitter's footprint; that a viewer must pay $.25 for each half hour of pay TV he watches; there is a two-way mechanism capable of charging for shows; and that there are twenty TV signals that compete on this basis. Assume, also, that all sets are turned on and that the television homes distribute themselves evenly among the channels. Further, assume that advertisers are willing to pay $.04 per home per half hour of viewing but that the pay signals have no commercials. If by switching to a "free" status one of the pay TV signals could thereby attract one-fourth of the viewers from each of the other nineteen signals (one last assumption), the free channel would have a viewership of 8.625 million homes and would earn revenues of $345,000 per half hour, while each pay channel would earn only $281,250 in that time. Clearly, at least one channel would switch to a free signal.

Would a second channel make the move? Suppose now that the addition of the second free channel would entice an additional 5 percent of the pay signal audience to start watching free TV, producing a total 30 percent drain on the viewership of each of the eighteen remaining pay stations. If the two free stations split this 30 percent equally, each would attract only 5.55 million homes and earn $222,000 in revenues per half hour, while each of the eighteen pay signals would have 1.05 million homes and earn $262,500 per half hour. Thus, the second signal's entry into the free TV market would be unlikely. Of course, changing the assumptions can change the result; a second, even a third free signal might be profitable. However, no reasonable manipulation of the assumptions would predict as many free signals as currently exist in major cities like New York, Los Angeles, or Chicago.

The above conclusion would gain force if the pay stations were to sell advertising, hoping to expand their revenue base. If all twenty pay TV operators in the example were to include advertising, each would earn $435,000 per half hour (1.5 million homes × $.25 + 1.5 million homes × $.04 = $375,000 + $60,000). Because the first free channel, we assume, would earn only $345,800 per half hour, no pay station would profit by changing its status. This conclusion rests on at least two important assumptions. First the demand for advertising time is perfectly elastic. In other words, broadcasters can sell as much advertising time as they want without lowering the price. Second, viewers regard a small number of commercials in their program as no cost at all. Relaxing the first assumption further dims the chances for free channels, while relaxing the second may brighten them. But however one modifies the assumptions, no reasonable analysis would predict more than a few free channels.*

Instead, there would probably be a mix of financing devices, much like those found in print today. Some newspapers, primarily weeklies, depend entirely on advertisers. Some periodicals, such as *Mad Magazine,* are financed almost exclusively by reader payments. The vast majority of publications, however, depend on both advertiser and reader payments. Similarly, an unfettered commercial television industry would probably include very few free signals, a few that were viewer-supported, and a large number supported by viewer and advertiser payments. To the extent that a decline in "free" stations reduced the availability of advertising space, advertising expenses would of course rise. If DBS stations provided advertising, the competition might reduce advertising prices.[29]

This short excursion into the economics of publishing and broadcasting has revealed nothing that justifies regulating broadcasting alone. Both media experience economies of scale in the transmission phase. Each poses the difficult question of

*R. NOLL, M. PECK & J. McGOWAN, ECONOMIC ASPECTS OF TELEVISION REGULATION 135 (1973), forcefully contend that converting the system of "free" television into pay television would reallocate massive amounts of consumer surplus to the licensees, program producers, and talent. (The FCC appears to be taking the first steps toward allowing just such a reallocation. *See,* 90 F.C.C.2d 341 (1982).) The welfare effects of shifting to a mixed system with many additional channels, but with fewer "free" channels, are much less clear.

Regardless of how such a welfare calculus comes out, the crucial question for this book is whether the calculus will be different for spectrum and paper. Although one might be tempted, as a first approximation, to presume that because the economics of broadcast and paper are so similar, the calculus would be the same, one would need to know more about consumer surplus in print and broadcast to be certain.

how best to deal with a naturally monopolistic bottleneck in the marketplace of ideas, and each requires that we choose between private ownership and some sort of public utility status. The market structures for print and broadcast, absent regulatory shaping, would probably resemble one another considerably.

Only one important difference emerges from my investigation. Broadcasting economies of scale have, to date, encompassed much larger geographic areas than newspaper economies. Taking advantage of these economies for a newspaper entails serving a metropolitan territory, but for a broadcaster means serving a multistate region. (Even this distinction, however, blurs with the emergence of nationwide satellite dailies, such as *USA Today* and the *Wall Street Journal*, both truly national newspapers.)

Does this difference justify different content control? Clearly not. Some might argue, however, that this difference justifies restricting the operating areas of broadcasters, so as to induce them to cater to the needs and interests of metropolitan areas, much as regional newspapers naturally do. This differential treatment would mimic current FCC regulations that restrict radio and television broadcasters to metropolitan territories. Because we have already shown that no scarcity argument requires such regulation, the regulation's proponent would have to argue that there is something special about metropolitan areas. The two most promising arguments center on building the area's sense of community and on nurturing the area's informed voting behavior. Each argument would require a great deal of support to be convincing.

Consider first building a sense of community. What can this mean in an area with several million inhabitants? Probably not that everyone has the same customs and beliefs. Instead, the several million inhabitants mostly share the media, the weather, and, to some extent, politics. To a large extent a sense of community is created by, as well as reported by, the media of mass communication. Might a multistate area develop a similar sense of community if it were served by the same broadcasters? A proponent of regulation would have to show it would not in order to justify his position.

Second, consider some basic questions about informed voting behavior, a topic expressly beyond the scope of this book. Do watching television and listening to the radio inform voters? If so, is it in a good way? Do voters alter their voting behavior based on this information? Do they vote more often? Are the changes, if any, good ones? Metropolitan areas correspond to senatorial and congressional jurisdictions better than multistate areas, but correspond worse to the presidential jurisdiction (the whole country). Are changes in voting behavior more or less important for the president, as opposed to the Senate and Congress? The proponent of regulation must answer these questions convincingly to justify his position. Until such answers are provided I will set aside this argument for content control.

What does all of this prove? In general, it shows that arguments based on industry structure apply just as well to print as they do to broadcast. Consequently, the content of the two media should, in most instances, be treated equally. This is not to say that some special circumstance might not demand a unique regulatory approach. The basic conclusion, however, is that when all industry structure considerations have been weighed and a certain regulation policy for print appears best, the analogous policy for broadcasting will likely also be best.

For example, consider the question of whether or not a candidate for elective office, attacked in either print or broadcast, should have a right to reply to the attack in the attacking publication. The Supreme Court has decided that although the state may not constitutionally afford a candidate a right of access to a newspaper, the FCC may constitutionally guarantee such access to broadcast stations. In general, however, the arguments for and against access apply equally well to both media. Imagine, for instance, a candidate attacked by one of the few papers in his region. To support his or her claim for a chance to respond, the candidate could claim that protecting the marketplace of ideas and the smooth functioning of democracy was more important than the publisher's liberty interests. The candidate could further claim that access to other publications within the umbrella industry structure (for example, competing regionals, locals, weeklies, or specialty publications) was inadequate. The newspaper publisher would contest each of these points, and would even suggest that other media, such as broadcast and cable TV, could provide suitable access to the public.

These arguments would apply equally well to a free-market broadcast industry like that hypothetically described earlier in this chapter. A candidate, attacked on one of the few "free" national television stations and seeking reply time, would claim that preserving the marketplace of ideas and effective democracy is more important than the broadcaster's liberty interests. He or she would further claim that access to other broadcast stations within the umbrella industry structure (for example, pay channels, regional terrestrials, weekenders, or radio) would not suffice. The broadcaster would contest each point, and suggest that other media, such as print and cable TV, could provide opportunity enough to reach the public.

This analysis does not grapple with the basic access conundrum. It only suggests that whatever form of access proves desirable for print should also be desirable for broadcast. Further, we should note that specific facts may vary the general result. To illustrate, a particular station may attract viewers who use no other news source, be it cable TV, over-the-air TV, newspapers, magazines, radio, or human conversation. As a result, the cross-medium substitution argument would not work for this particular station. Such scenarios, however, are likely to be rare and idiosyncratic. They would require careful analysis and cannot be adequately anticipated. Consequently, I return to the basic conclusion: there is no justification, based on industry structure, for controlling content in broadcasting differently from that in print.

The Modern Argument: Promoting First Amendment Values

T HE modern argument, put forth by Lee Bollinger, professor of law at the University of Michigan, appeals directly to first amendment norms rather than to economic efficiency. However, because this argument is so intertwined with industry structure it is appropriate to discuss it here.

THE ARGUMENT

Bollinger[1] contends that, although there are *no* relevant differences between printed publications and broadcasting, we should, as a matter of first amendment theory, treat print and broadcast differently through partial access regulation—regulating access to one of these media in the way access to broadcast is currently regulated.[2] Bollinger refers to the panoply of content restrictions on broadcasting—including the fairness doctrine, the equal time provisions for personal attacks, and so forth—as access regulations, and he calls a system wherein one medium, but not others, operates under them a system of "partial" access. Bollinger supports this position with the following argument: the first amendment is designed to serve a panoply of goals, including protecting the smooth functioning of the marketplace of ideas and the proper functioning of democracy. These values can be threatened not only by untoward government action, but also by highly concentrated private media, for in such circumstances the private media owners may deny individuals access. By enforcing a system of partial

43

access regulation we can increase the net satisfaction of first amendment goals.

Bollinger argues that there are intangible benefits from a system of access regulation imposed on all media:

> An access rule is designed to operate in the service of the first amendment. It seeks to neutralize the disparities that impede the proper functioning of the "market-place of ideas," to equalize opportunities within our society to command an audience and thereby to mobilize public opinion, and in that sense to help realize democratic ideals.[3]

Note that Bollinger's description of the benefits from regulation can usefully be divided into access and diversity. Access refers to a speaker's ability to address an audience—"opportunities within our society to command an audience." Diversity denotes the multiplicity of offerings to the audience—"the proper functioning of the 'market-place of ideas.'"

However, Bollinger continues, access regulation also threatens to be very costly. It may, first of all, discourage the press (both print and broadcast) from covering controversy at all, for when an outlet questions the honesty, character, or integrity of a person or group while covering a controversial subject, members of the audience must be given access to the outlet's facilities. Under the current scheme of broadcast regulation, for example, the attacked members must be given use of the facilities even if the attack upon their honesty, character, or integrity was completely true.[4] (This both deprives the owner of the use of the facilities, and may cost the owner some readers/viewers if the responding speaker says or prints content objectionable to the outlet's regular audience). Second, it may produce an administrative machine that will inevitably abuse discretion and force the regulated press into an official line, thereby interfering with the "checking" function of the press.[5] And third, it may start a slide down a slippery slope to more intrusive, more objectionable regulation.[6]

Bollinger argues that a system of partial regulation may reduce the possible costs attending access regulation. First, an unregulated press will continue to cover controversy.[7] In a similar vein, the government will be unable effectively to suppress the truth or any criticism of the government because the unregulated sector will continue to provide the information. And, in general, the existence of the unregulated sector of the press will provide a competitive prod to the regulated sector, thereby preventing the regulated sector from giving in to government desires, and serving as a reminder of the dangers of sliding down the slippery slope to more intrusive regulation.

We have treated broadcast as the regulated medium, Bollinger argues, but we need not continue to do so. Congress should be allowed to reverse its field, Bollinger continues, and regulate newspapers, at least to some extent, if it stops regulating broadcast.

> Instead, the Court ought to acknowledge broadcasters as full-fledged participants in our first amendment traditions and yet permit Congress to engage in *some* experimentation with press freedom to facilitate public access, allowing Congress to choose the medium to be regulated. This means, of course, that eventually the legislative branch may shift the target of its regulatory scheme to other segments of the media, provided it abandons its earlier target. Thus, it ought theoretically to be possible for Congress to abandon its regulation of the electronic media and choose instead to provide access within the confines of the newspaper industry.[8]

CRITIQUE

Bollinger's argument relies on the *systemic* benefits from freedom of expression. Freedom of speech and press are prized because they inform the electorate within a democracy and help to produce, through the "marketplace of ideas," useful ideas for the improvement of society, scientific advancement, and so forth. However, there is another set of arguments, based on individual freedom and autonomy, for freedom of expression. These arguments characterize freedom of speech and press as necessary for the autonomous individual to constitute himself as a whole, healthy personality.[9]

My critique of Bollinger's argument presumes, for the most part, that Bollinger's systemic approach to the first amendment is correct, but shows that, given his basic premises, his argument fails.*

Bollinger's Argument Leads to a Different Conclusion

Assuming that regulation effectively enhances access and diversity, Bollinger's concerns about these goals still do not suggest regulating one of the media and not the other. By regulating all broadcasters but not all printed publications, the current system skews the distribution of values served in favor of those people who strongly prefer receiving one medium or the other. For example, those who cannot read, and who therefore strongly prefer broadcast, will be confined to the values of fair but homogenized communication. Conversely, those who live in areas unserved by broadcast may be confined to interesting but biased publications because none are subject to the fairness doctrine. Because millions of people cannot read[10] and many own no television set,[11] these effects are very important.

Of course, virtually all content-neutral restrictions have similar effects. If the state were to prohibit leafletting at a state fair, for example, in order to control traffic flow and prevent litter, those who prefer to attend the fair would have reduced

---

*The discussion of access, but not diversity, can be read as appealing to both systemic and individualistic rationales for free expression. If we were to concentrate on the individualistic arguments for free expression Bollinger's argument would likely fare no better. For example, why would it be better to allow newspaper publishers to express their personalities, free of government control, but deny this opportunity to those who wished to broadcast? If there are good reasons for having some regulated media outlets, it would be better to have some regulated and some unregulated outlets in both print and broadcast. This argument parallels exactly the argument in chapter 4.

access to information compared to those who have other preferences. As long as the state has other good reasons for the regulation and is not motivated by a desire to restrict the flow of information to fairgoers, the courts will uphold the law. Here, however, the very reason for partial regulation is to enforce first amendment values on behalf of the public. In this context, skewing the distribution of first amendment values to one group or another must be crucial, for there is no other purpose to justify the regulations.[12]

Bollinger's argument would suggest creating two classes of broadcasters and print publishers. Every geographic area of the country would have some licensed newspapers, subject to content controls, and some unlicensed newspapers, free from controls. Broadcasters would be similarly divided. In this fashion, those who cannot read would be exposed to the full panoply of first amendment values, as would those who live in areas unserved by broadcast. If broadcast and print were fungible in all respects, it would make sense to license one entire medium and not the other. But because the media do not serve identical groups, Bollinger's argument does not work.

Nor can Bollinger reconstruct his argument by claiming that political realities make licensing newspapers impossible. Such a response would fail because a retreat to political feasibility can trump all analysis, including his own. Politics may now have cemented licensed broadcasters, as well as unlicensed newspapers, onto the political landscape. Further, if politics only precludes licensing newspapers, but allows deregulation of some broadcasters, Bollinger's argument reduces to an argument for two classes of broadcasters (licensed and unlicensed), not the radically different treatment of the media in place today.

Also, note that Bollinger's proposal seems to trigger the traditional prohibition on content regulation. His proposal seems to allow the Congress to give no reason at all for choosing to regulate one or another of the media. Unbridled discretion in government officials to control speakers or a medium of expression has traditionally been treated as a form of content control, forbidden by the first amendment.[13]

My reconstruction of Bollinger's argument—regulated and unregulated sections within each of the media—may be unworkable without a system of subsidies. The current system of access regulation is costly for those who must labor under it. If one merely unleashed both regulated and unregulated newspapers and broadcasters competing side by side in markets, the regulated firms would earn lower profits than their unregulated counterparts. This closely resembles the problems faced by AT&T today. It is required simultaneously to subsidize local telephone service from the revenues of long-distance service, and to face competition from companies that have no such duty. This allows competing companies to charge lower prices.[14]

An attempt to sell a new issue of stock in a regulated newspaper or broadcaster that must function in competitive markets might be impossible. Investors would not put their money into an enterprise that promised less than competitive returns if alternatives were available. To persuade investors to put capital into one of these regulated enterprises, the government would have to subsidize the regulated newspapers and broadcasters.

This subsidy could be granted in at least two different ways. First, the government could auction off some very large capital assets, such as spectrum bands or printing plants, subject to the restriction that the capital assets must be used to produce regulated newspapers or broadcasts. Because regulation is costly, the value of the assets would fall, compared to their value in unregulated use. But as long as the capitalized cost of regulation does not exceed the value of the assets in unregulated use, the value of the assets would not fall to zero and someone would use the assets.

The alternative approach would involve giving the regulated firms annual cash subsidies. This approach seems far less preferable because, of course, it brings up all of the issues traditionally involved in public utility ratemaking: How large should the subsidy be? How large are "normal" profits? Should profits be measured with respect to what ideal management could have accomplished? Or with respect to what average management could have accomplished? How should one treat construction work in progress? And so forth. This list of questions should cause even the most ardent supporter of access to pause before embracing this second approach to giving subsidies.

I have now contrasted three basic systems: free market, partial regulation divided along media lines (as with the status quo), and partial regulation within each medium. We have seen that shifting from a market system to partial regulation divided along media lines creates the added costs of skewing the distribution of first amendment values to the public. In contrast, moving instead to partial regulation within each medium requires subsidizing the regulated firms. A system of partial regulation is preferable to a market system only if a system of partial regulation produces valuable enough benefits to outweigh the costs of regulation. And even in such circumstances, partial regulation divided along media lines (the status quo) would be preferable to partial regulation within each medium only if we discount the costs of skewing the distribution of first amendment values served to the public, and only if we also regard both methods of subsidy to be very costly, so that subsidy costs outweigh the status quo's first amendment costs. However, I have already shown that the second of these conclusions is unreasonable—partial access regulation divided along media lines causes large costs, and there would be a relatively inexpensive subsidy method for partial regulation within each medium. I will now show that the benefits from the current system of partial regulation are small, if not nonexistent, and will also introduce a fourth system, common carrier, that would provide greater net benefits than the current system of partial regulation. The common carrier system would treat print and broadcast equally.

Current Regulation Provides Few Benefits, Especially Compared to a Common Carrier System

The current system of partial access regulation produces few benefits, for two important reasons. First, partial regulation provides much less protection against governmental tampering with the media, both regulated and unregulated, than Bollinger claims. Second, Bollinger justifies the current system of partial access regulation entirely by the supposed increases in access and diversity that it achieves. However, the current system of access regulation for broadcasters does not clearly increase either access or diversity and may substantially decrease both, compared to that which would be produced by a free market. Because Bollinger's argument is anchored in the current system of partial access regulation, I will first discuss that system, and then analyze a common carrier system.

Partial regulation provides much less protection against governmental tampering with the media than it otherwise might because more and more frequently one company owns broadcasting stations, newspapers, and magazines. This allows the government to punish a broadcasting station's parent corporation for misbehavior by its unregulated subsidiary. Consider this transcript of a conversation in the White House:

> SPECIAL ASSISTANT JOHN DEAN: The [Washington] Post, as you know, has got a real large team that they've assigned to do nothing but this [Watergate case]. Couldn't believe they put Maury Stans' [a Nixon cabinet member and later a Nixon fund raiser] story about his libel suit, which was just playing so heavily on the networks last night, and in the evening news, they put it way back on about page eight of the Post. . . .
>
> PRESIDENT NIXON: I expect that. That's all right. We've [Unintelligible].
>
> SPECIAL ASSISTANT H.R. HALDEMAN: The Post is—
>
> PRESIDENT: The Post has asked—it's going to have its problems.
>
> DEAN: The networks, the networks are good with Maury coming back three days in a row and—
>
> PRESIDENT: That's right. Right. The main thing is the Post is going to have damnable, damnable problems out of this one. They have a television station—
>
> DEAN: That's right, they do.

PRESIDENT: And they're going to have to get it renewed.

HALDEMAN: They've got a radio station, too.

PRESIDENT: Does that come up too? The point is, when does it come up?

DEAN: I don't know. But the practice of nonlicensees filing on top of licensees has certainly gotten more—

PRESIDENT: That's right.

DEAN: More active in the, in the area.

PRESIDENT: And it's going to be goddamn active here.[15]

Thus partial regulation allows government interference to spread into the unregulated sector. A common carrier system, discussed at the end of this section, would avoid this problem.

Next, consider the failure of the current system to substantially increase access or diversity. Before proceeding with this analysis, however, I should define "access" and "diversity" more precisely. For purposes of this discussion, access is the ability of any individual in a particular market to place his message within the reach of the audience. Note that in a market with several media outlets, this definition does not require that an individual be able to get time or space on any particular outlet, as long as one is available.

An alternative definition of access is the ability of an individual to reach the listeners or readers of a particular station or print publication.[16] (There is, in general, no such right of access under the current system of regulation of broadcast.[17]) We will not use this second definition because doing so would defeat Bollinger's argument immediately. Because access to radio or television stations cannot provide access to particular print publications, a partial system similar to the status quo cannot suffice. If we were to conclude that some form of access regulation was needed for broadcast, we would be impelled to conclude the same about print. Therefore, I will use the first definition of access given above—the ability of any individual to put his message within the reach of listeners or viewers within a given media market.[18]

Diversity, the other value involved in this set of arguments, refers to the heterogeneity of material produced in any given market: The more types of programming or writing produced in any given market, the more diversity there is. Measurement of diversity depends on the taxonomy of possible types and the classification of a program as a particular type. Because these measures are somewhat subjective and vague, the measurement of diversity is highly imprecise. Notwithstanding this problem, diversity captures the value to the audience of being able to choose its favorite type of material. Bruce Owen has shown that there is no necessary general relationship between diversity and viewer welfare.[19] However, if one makes some assumptions about the preferences of viewers—that they derive great pleasure from getting access to their favorite type of program, but derive little additional joy from gaining access to an additional choice of an already available type—then diversity and viewer welfare do tend to correlate. The more diversity in a media market, the happier consumers are. To see this, consider an example in which there are only three types of program—news, sporting events, and situation comedies—and three television stations. Each viewer has a favorite type of program, cares intensely about gaining access to his favorite type, but cares little about having access to a second or third version of his favorite. Those who like situation comedies will be very happy to have access to one sitcom, but will be made only slightly happier to have access to a second sitcom. And those who love news or sporting events have similar feelings about their own favorites. If this market has one news show, one sporting event, and one sitcom on the air at any given time, consumers will be better off than if any one type of program were to be neglected entirely and, instead, two versions of one of the others were to be shown. In this way diversity can produce greater consumer happiness. The main exceptions to this type of analysis are campaign messages from candidates. A varied diet of these is widely regarded as political castor oil—good for the people regardless of their pleasure.

Access and diversity are closely related. The more access there is to a media market, the more one can expect the market to produce diverse offerings. The more diverse the offerings are in a market, the better the evidence is that the market provides good access. Together, access and diversity represent the two sides of the marketplace of ideas, and their fundamental interdependence precludes discussing one without the other. Therefore, I will discuss these two values together.

The concept of broadcaster "fairness"—requiring broadcasters to cover controversial issues in an evenhanded manner and to allow all types of politicians to have access to their facilities during campaigns—is implicit in current regulation, but it adds nothing extra to our analysis. Fairness cannot, by itself, justify differential content control. If fairness is good because it produces a mix of unfair and fair, represented by newspapers and broadcasters, then fairness cannot justify regulation; the free market produces a mix of fairness and unfairness in print today and would undoubtedly do so in a free market in broadcast. If, instead, fairness is valued because it ensures that *every* broadcaster is fair, then it is impossible to explain, without some additional argument, why newspapers should not also be fair. Therefore, I will ignore fairness as an independent value that can justify differential content control, and concentrate on the more basic values of access and diversity.

The following argument will show that Bollinger's argument fails because: (1) a media market with a large number of outlets will almost certainly produce a more diverse mix of material than does the current system of access regulation in broadcasting; (2) a media market with a large number of outlets will probably give at least as much access as does the current system; and (3) a media market with few outlets will not clearly outperform or underperform the current system, but in such a market the proper response (if any) would be to set up some sort of common carrier system in both print and broadcast, rather than maintain the current system of access regulation.

The market, access, and the production of diversity.   A broadcast market with few outlets will tend to produce uniform programming. First, assume that viewers tend to have many different types of first-choice programming. These might be sporting events, ballet, rock concerts, opera, origami lessons, and so forth. Most viewers will be willing to watch common denominator programming, for example, "Dynasty," if their first choice is not shown. Second, assume that broadcasters wish to make as much profit as they can and, because advertisers pay more to communicate with larger groups, the broadcasters attempt to maximize the size of their audiences. Because profit-maximizing broadcasters compete with one another, they make their programming choices based, in part, on the programming choices of their competitors. If there are only two competitors, each would probably find it in his interest to program mass appeal, common denominator programming. If one broadcaster airs these programs, such as "Dynasty," the other will have to choose between airing specialty programming—opera—or more mass appeal programming—"Dallas." The first assumption implies that if the second broadcaster airs opera, it will garner a tiny percentage (for example, 5 percent) of the viewing audience, leaving a very large audience for the first broadcaster, because many of the remaining 95 percent who are uninterested in opera will watch the only available mass-appeal program. But if the second broadcaster programs "Dallas," it can get approximately 50 percent of the viewers—a much more profitable result. If the first broadcaster had programmed specialty matter, it obviously would be in the interest of the second broadcaster to counter with mass-appeal programming, thereby taking the lion's share of the audience. This model shows that it will always be in the interest of both broadcasters to air mass appeal, common denominator programming.[20] Nothing much changes if there are three broadcasters, rather than two. This is the standard explanation for the overwhelming sameness of network television programming.

On the other hand, if there are many competing outlets, the market will produce substantial diversity. To see this, change the example above so that there are twenty-five competing broadcasters. If all twenty-five program mass appeal, common denominator programming, each can expect roughly 4 percent of the viewing audience. In these circumstances it will be in the interest of one broadcaster to counter with opera, garnering 5 percent of the audience. (Recall that 5 percent of the audience prefers opera to all other choices.) This process will continue until it is no longer profitable to switch from mass appeal to specialty programming. In general, increasing the number of broadcasters segments the viewership for mass appeal programming so much that the small audiences for specialty programming appear competitive. Once specialty programming is competitive, the market will produce a highly diverse mix.

The recent case of *Cosmopolitan Broadcasting Corp. v. FCC*[21] illustrates this process within a market with many competitors. Cosmopolitan operated an FM radio station, WHBI, licensed to serve Newark, New Jersey. This market competes with New York City, where there are many radio stations. WHBI first failed to make a profit when it broadcast black-oriented material.[22] WHBI then switched strategies, and by 1969 was selling most of its air time in large chunks to "time brokers." These brokers resold the time in smaller chunks, mostly to foreign-language and ethnic-specialty programmers but also to individuals, in five-minute chunks between 3:00 A.M. and 6:00 A.M. As a result, 68 percent of WHBI's programming presented material in eighteen foreign languages, including Spanish, Italian, Greek, Hungarian, Arabic, Polish, Brazilian, Portuguese, Lithuanian, Slovakian, Croatian, Bulgarian, and Norwegian.[23] By 1972 WHBI also broadcast programming in Korean, Macedonian, Urdu, Hindi, Bengali, Japanese, and Russian. Unfortunately for Cosmopolitan, the FCC prohibits time brokering. Instead, the FCC requires each broadcaster to be a fiduciary for the listening public and to program for the public interest in its service area. Time brokering, with its consequent loss of control, violates the spirit of the fiduciary model.[24] Therefore, Cosmopolitan's broadcasting license was not renewed.

The facts of *Cosmopolitan Broadcasting* provide striking insight into diversity produced by access under a market system. To gain access to the listening public, one need not purchase an entire broadcasting station. Instead, one could buy a small slice of time. Time brokers could specialize in reselling small chunks of time to would-be programmers, thereby greatly reducing transaction costs. As a result, many new programmers could gain access. For example, commercial minutes were being sold for as little as $5 on WHBI.[25] The ultimate product could be a very diverse mix, as with the foreign-language programming comprising the bulk of WHBI's schedule.

Our current system of access regulation in broadcast, in contrast, may provide less diversity than would an unregulated market. There are four basic reasons: rules against time brokering, rules against multiple network affiliations, the enforcement of the fairness doctrine, and the stingy allocation of spectrum to television broadcasting.

The rules against time brokering raise the costs of presenting material from producers who wish to reach very limited audiences. This is shown by the example of WHBI. Time brokers specialize in finding the programmers and then helping them make programming decisions and deal with broadcasters. If time brokering is outlawed, then the individual stations must hire the time brokers to do the various tasks, making them, in effect, managers. This reduces efficiency in at least three ways. First, if the station tries to hire a time broker to deal with all the different programmers, he will likely be less efficient at dealing with most of them than were the specialist time brokers. Second, if the station hires several time broker specialists it may be forced to purchase more hours of their time than it really requires. Finally, the station will be forced to bear the risk of not selling blocks of time. Stations want to sell time brokers large blocks of time because the brokers are superior risk bearers. When the brokers are employees, however, they lose their incentive to manage risk as effectively. These reductions in efficiency raise the costs of dealing with small programmers and enhance the attractiveness of buying prepackaged radio formats from syndicators.

The FCC has a rule preventing a broadcaster from affiliating with more than one network[26] that applies if there is any unaffiliated station licensed to its area, no matter how poorly that station may be received. This rule prevents new, fringe networks, designed to cater to specialized audiences, from getting started because often all desirable broadcasters in an area have already affiliated with an established network (ABC, CBS, NBC).[27] This rule may also handicap a small station that wishes to affiliate with several smaller networks, producing, in effect, a "magazine" format. Again, the net result is probably less diversity.

The fairness doctrine requires broadcasters to cover controversial issues in an evenhanded manner, but the manner in which it is applied probably reduces diversity. As Thomas Krattenmaker and Lucas Powe have recently shown in *The Fairness Doctrine Today: A Constitutional Curiosity and an Impossible Dream*,[28] the FCC devotes virtually no resources to monitoring fairness doctrine compliance, responding mainly to citizen complaints of station bias in covering an issue. Because defending a fairness complaint is very costly, stations have an economic incentive to avoid entirely covering controversy. By doing so they cheaply avoid all fairness doctrine complaints, but reduce diversity in the marketplace.

The rules against time brokering and limiting affiliation are embedded within a rather stingy allocation of spectrum to television broadcasting. This has tended to produce many markets with very few television stations, which in turn reduces access for speakers and produces a homogeneous output for the audience. As discussed above, in markets with few broadcasters there will be a tendency for broadcasters to aim for the great middle. In such circumstances, broadcasters may also refuse to sell slices of time to fringe speakers because of fear of offending the regular audience.[29]

Focusing on access. A supporter of the current system might respond, at this point, "I understand that the FCC might reduce access in some ways, but at least we have the fairness doctrine and other safeguards to ensure that opposing points of view are aired. Under a market system a powerful interest might buy all of the time to keep a fringe speaker off the air." A fringe speaker will be defined as an individual or group whose message is unpopular with the majority of the audience in the market and whose finances are limited. The foreign-language programmers on WHBI were fringe speakers (because their programming was unpopular with most listeners); most listeners probably changed stations when programming in Urdu was aired. I will spend little time worrying about the ability of middle-of-the-road, well-financed speakers to gain access, for they will likely have a great deal of access under a market system.

A simple example demonstrates that the strategy of buying all of the air time so as to exclude a fringe speaker would be very expensive and unlikely to succeed, even in a rather concentrated market. Assume that there are only five radio stations in a given market. These radio stations are on the air all the time, so there are a total of (24 hrs /day)×(7 days/wk)×(5 stations)=840 hrs/wk of air time. Assume that all hours have an equal market value of $100 and that all hours are sold. Then, radio sponsors are spending $84,000 per week. Assume further that there is a fringe speaker who wants to spend $500 per week on radio time, and so expects to broadcast for 5 hours per week. A wealthy enemy of the fringe speaker would have to spend a great deal of money to keep the fringe speaker off the air. The enemy could not offer $101 per hour and buy all of the time, for the fringe speaker could then offer $102 per hour and buy at least $4\frac{3}{4}$ hours. The enemy must offer at least $500 per hour for all of the broadcast hours so as to preclude the fringe speaker from access. But this would entail an expenditure of ($500/hr)×(840 hrs/wk)=$420,000/wk. (As I will show below, if the enemy tried to resell the time at monopoly rates he would be subject to treble damages and criminal penalties under the antitrust laws.) The strategy of precluding fringe speakers by purchasing air time seems too expensive to succeed. Further, if the strategy succeeded at first, radio stations in this market would make a very high return on investment, and this would tend to attract entry by another radio station into the market. An entrepreneur would purchase the rights to another frequency in the market and shift that frequency into radio broadcast, thereby providing the fringe speaker with another outlet for access.

Could the enemy spend less and just reduce, rather than

eliminate, the fringe speaker's access? Yes, but doing so would also be very expensive, considering the results. For the enemy to limit the fringe speaker to 4 hours per week—only a 20 percent reduction—the price of air time would have to rise to $125 per hour. At this price, radio sponsors (including the enemy) would have to spend at least ($125/hr)×(840 hrs /wk)= $105,000/wk. Of course, the regular radio sponsors might purchase some of the hours, even at $125 per hour, but unless demand for time were quite inelastic the enemy would have to foot a great deal of the bill. And even in this circumstance, the fringe speaker would still broadcast for 4 hours. Last, the strategy of buying up all or a part of the time would be no more attractive in a market with only one broadcaster. It would still be extremely expensive and ineffective.

All of the enemy's alternative strategies,[30] which might appear at first blush more effective, would be blatant violations of the antitrust laws, easily detected, and punished by treble damages plus awards of attorneys fees to prevailing litigants. (This should surprise no one, because, for the most part, policies that promote competition among the media also promote first amendment values.[31]) In addition, the alternative strategies also would be very expensive.

For example, if the enemy were simply to buy all of the radio stations and then refuse to sell time to the fringe speaker, he would be guilty of monopolization under the Sherman Act.[32] Buying all of the radio stations also would be very expensive, especially if any of their current owners were to learn of the enemy's plan and hold him up for a high price. In addition, monopolization would be easy to detect. If, instead, the enemy were to contract with each of the five radio stations not to sell time to the fringe speaker, the enemy (and the radio stations) would be guilty of a group boycott,[33] a horizontal restraint of trade, prohibited under the Sherman Act. Further, the enemy would have to pay each of the radio stations at least $501 per week in exchange for the promise, resulting in an outlay of at least $2,505 per week. And every radio station would have to extract a promise from each of its customers not to resell its purchased time to the fringe speaker, thereby involving large numbers of parties in this conspiracy and making it easy to discover.

Are there any situations in which private parties might have difficulty gaining access to unregulated media markets? Yes, but as the discussion below will show, these problems provide support not for the current system of access regulation, but rather for some sort of common carrier system.

A broadcaster would likely refuse a fringe speaker access for one of two reasons: either because the fringe speaker's message would disturb the broadcaster's audience, or because the broadcaster disagrees with the fringe speaker. Both of these reasons are far more likely to gain importance as both market concentration and the perceived odiousness of the speaker's message rise. First, consider the audience. Recall that if there are only a few broadcasters in the market, the medium is advertiser-supported, most viewers are willing to watch common-denominator, mass-appeal programming, and viewers who are willing to watch mass-appeal programming dislike fringe messages, then each broadcaster will program for the great middle audience—those with average tastes and a dislike for fringe messages.[34] If there are many broadcasters, then some will find it profitable to program so as to reach audiences who will listen to fringe messages.[35] Hence, a market with more broadcasters provides more access to a fringe speaker.

There is one possible, albeit unlikely, exception to this analysis. If there is only one broadcaster in a market, and most viewers will continue to view television regardless of what is broadcast, the single broadcaster need not fear offending its viewers with fringe messages. Thus, the broadcaster may be willing to sell time to fringe speakers. However, if there are at least two broadcasters in the market, or if viewers offended by fringe messages turn off their sets, then the original analysis holds; decreasing concentration in the media market alleviates access problems. Because the latter scenarios are far more likely, I will ignore the possibility that high concentration produces more access.

Second, consider personal disagreement. Broadcasters might refuse to air a speaker's message because the broadcaster strongly disagrees with the message, or because there is a shared norm, evolving out of consciously parallel behavior, that one does not air messages that aggravate one's fellow broadcasters. Obviously, a market with more broadcasters will more likely contain one who does not refuse to air a fringe speaker's message based on personal feelings. And such a market will be less likely to foster the evolution of shared norms and parallel behavior. Hence, the more broadcasters there are in a given market, the less likely are their personal feelings to interfere with access for fringe messages.

Political candidate access. There is one elite group, however, that almost certainly enjoys greater access to the airwaves, particularly in concentrated markets, because of current regulation. Federal statutes guarantee candidates for federal elective office "reasonable" access to broadcast facilities. In addition, when a broadcaster allows a candidate, whether for federal, state, or local office, to use his station he must give all other candidates in the same race equal time, under equal terms and conditions. The combination of these two rules clearly eases federal elective candidates' task of getting air time; the broadcasters have virtually no choice but to agree to requests.

These rules raise some interesting questions. Why are only candidates for federal office guaranteed access? Does this not suggest an unhealthy relationship between the regulated medium and the regulators? Do the equal time rules impede access to the airwaves for candidates to state and local offices?

These rules may not substantially increase the overall diversity of offerings within the market. In markets with many broadcasters, most candidates would probably get access even without the current rules. In markets with few broadcasters, current rules may increase the diversity of announcements from candidates for federal office, but the diversity of messages from state and local candidates shrinks correspondingly. By denying access to the first nonfederal candidate, a broadcaster can avoid the duty of affording equal time to all others. As broadcasters are required to sell time to federal candidates they are likely to attempt to control the disruption in their schedules by selling less time to nonfederal candidates.

These rules also suggest an unhealthy relationship between the regulators and the regulated. If Congress had truly been concerned with the "public interest" in elections, it probably would have guaranteed state and local candidates access as well. A skeptic would conclude that Congress extended access rights no farther because congressmen and senators were concerned solely with their own reelection races.

The current system increases access for candidates for federal office because broadcasters have virtually no choice but to agree to a request. At the same time, the current system's drawbacks stem from the failure to extend this mandatory access approach to others. The next section will consider a common carrier system that would extend these principles and broadly guarantee a certain degree of access.

Pulling it all together. In sum, the crucial issue with respect to access and diversity is whether there are enough broadcasters in the market. If there are many broadcasters, one can expect the market to produce a much more diverse mix than the current system does. Similarly, in markets with many broadcasters the possible problem of access provides no justification for the current regulations. A few speakers with the most unpopular messages may still have trouble gaining access within such a market. But the current system of broadcast regulation generally gives such groups no right of access anyway, so such access problems do not argue for the status quo.

In more concentrated markets, comparing the market with the current system of regulation is much less clear. The market may not produce a diverse mix of programming, but neither does the current system. And there may be an access problem in the free market, but it likely would be no worse than under the current system. Only candidates for federal elective office, a group generally undeserving of much solicitude, gain from the current system. Candidates for state and local office appear to lose.

The overall comparison is quite clear. The market would

outperform the current system in unconcentrated markets and probably do as well as the current system in concentrated markets. Therefore, the current system of access regulation should be rejected.

Perhaps, one might counter, we should just allocate more spectrum to broadcasting, repeal the restrictions on time brokering and network affiliation, keep partial access regulation in broadcasting, and forgo the market solution. Such a suggestion should be rejected for at least two reasons. First, the political economy of broadcast regulation suggests that administrative rules limiting access will evolve. Second, even in markets so concentrated that some form of access regulation should be employed, the better response would be to adopt some form of common carrier system.

There are political temptations to use the administrative machinery to limit access in just the ways Bollinger fears. The FCC restricts the number of broadcast licenses, thereby giving them great value. It then awards these licenses without charge, but subject to renewal, so that licensees have a great interest in conforming to the rules. The Congress creates and funds the FCC, which in turn has a great interest in pleasing Congress. The FCC has responded by awarding licenses to many small, local stations,[36] thereby maximizing the number of stations and assigning them to many congressional districts.[37] Congressmen, who regard broadcasters as both conduits to their constituents and as sources of jobs and revenue for their districts, like this. The FCC has also promulgated rules against time brokering and affiliating with more than one network, thus centering responsibility for what is broadcast onto a few individuals. The broadcasters, not wishing to offend those who grant the licenses, voluntarily tone down criticism of elected officials. This dynamic culminated, for example, in the CBS network's famous decision to cancel the "Smothers Brothers Show." The show that triggered cancellation included a segment in which Dan Rowan, a guest star, attempted to give the "flying fickle finger of fate" to Senator John Pastore, then a member of the Senate Commerce Committee—the FCC's oversight committee in the Senate. Rather than risk angering the powerful Senator Pastore, CBS canceled an otherwise profitable show.[38]

The current system of access regulation, a product of the political and economic forces just described, fails to respond to Bollinger's concerns for several reasons. First, the requirements are vague enough to defy good enforcement, leading the FCC to rely instead upon the good faith and discretion of broadcasters, and to find very seldom that a broadcaster has violated the fairness doctrine.[39] Second, many of the requirements for giving access are contingent on having provided access to someone else—thereby blunting any incentive to give the first person access.[40] Last, the broadcasters rely on licenses that can be awarded to others at renewal time under rather vague criteria.[41]

Common carrier regulation could shelter broadcast access from these political and economic forces. A common carrier system could, for example, locate a broadcast station in each market and provide access to all under a tariffed basis, with no ability to discriminate. If someone wished to broadcast a program, he or she could purchase some time from the common carrier station, which would have no choice but to broadcast the program without any change. If need be, the rates of a broadcast common carrier could be controlled just as the prices of a public utility are regulated.[42] Such a common carrier, competing side by side with non-common carriers, would labor under a severe handicap if it could neither edit nor arrange content. The overall product would likely be less appealing and hence garner a much smaller audience. Because advertisers would pay little for time during a sparsely watched program, the production costs would have to be paid for either from charges to speakers or from some other source, such as tax revenues.

Of course, some will claim that access to a sparsely watched station does not fulfill the value of access and that private media must have a common carrier obligation to carry messages. If such common carrier messages were segregated, either by time, in the case of broadcast, or by specified pages, in the case of print, and if the carrier could not edit or arrange the material, audiences for those portions would probably shrink. If 6:00 to 7:00 P.M. were set aside as the common carrier hour on a local broadcast station, many fewer people would watch that station from 6:00 to 7:00 P.M. Similarly, if part 6 of the local newspaper carried the common carrier copy, fewer people would read part 6. However, if all broadcasters and newspapers were to labor under such a burden, none would need to be subsidized in the ways described at the beginning of this chapter.

The argument would likely be carried further—that there must be access to all portions of all private media. But such a claim clearly stands upon the discarded notion of access: the ability to put one's message before a particular audience. Recall that Bollinger's argument failed quickly when I used this definition.[43] Further, such a notion of access runs directly counter to any notion of privacy—the right not to hear or read unwanted messages[44]—and therefore might be rejected directly on the merits. But any one of these common carrier systems would avoid the major pitfalls of the current system. In each, the broadcaster would have neither the ability nor the incentive to blunt criticism of the government or fail to cover controversy. Further, there would be no favoritism for federal candidates. State and local candidates could gain access on an equal basis. However, because the print and broadcast industries are likely to have the same structure, common carrier type obligations would be applied to both media, or to neither, in the same general fashion.[45]

One last nagging question may remain: Under either a pure market system or one including common carriers that are not completely subsidized, would fringe speakers be able to afford both print and broadcast? The answer depends on what the fringe speaker wants. A minute on network television during prime time or a full page in *Time* magazine would lie beyond the average person's budget, but a couple of minutes on a local radio station or six column inches in the local newspaper would be quite affordable. If, for some reason, we were to decide that this would not be enough, direct cash grants to some speakers could help. However, remember that no system can banish economic scarcity and give all speakers unlimited access.

In sum, Bollinger's argument for partial access regulation fails for three reasons. First, his own argument would not lead to different treatment *of the media.* Second, the market generally provides access as good as that provided by the current system. Last, common carrier obligations are almost certainly superior to the current system of access regulation in broadcast and would apply (or not) equally well to both media.

II Rationales about Effects on Viewers

TWO different types of arguments for regulating broadcast (principally television)[1] more strictly than print assert that, of the two media, the former is more prone to affect its audience detrimentally. One type contends that, through its very technology, television improperly affects viewers' ideas, but reading, in contrast, does no such thing. The second type focuses instead on the presumed tendency of certain broadcast material to inspire "bad" behavior. Bad behavior, in its broadest sense, could include both that which is universally condemned (such as sexual assault), as well as that which is actually championed by large groups of people (such as certain voting patterns). However, I will examine only the first category. Thus, I will consider sexually explicit and violent material, concentrating on these materials' supposed ability to inspire antisocial behavior. I will also ask related questions about accessibility to children. I selected these areas because they fuel two of the most visible, emotionally charged, and potentially persuasive rationales for regulating content.

Several areas are left unexplored. One might, for example, investigate the effects of broadcasting on voters' and candidates' political participation; on consumers' consumption patterns;[2] on prejudicial stereotyping; or on children's learning patterns and capabilities.[3] Should the investigation disclose unwanted characteristics of broadcasting, it is important to remember that this, in itself, would not justify differential regulation. Such justification would depend on proof that these concerns do not equally apply to print, that is, that reading the same content does not induce the very same bad behavior.

4 Television and Improper Persuasion

O NE rationale for regulating television differently from print rests on purported psychological differences between watching television and reading.[1] According to this rationale, television induces uncritical acceptance of its messages, exerting an hypnotic effect on viewers and bypassing the analytical portion of the brain.

THE BASIC ARGUMENT

First, proponents argue that television is less involving than print.[2] A medium is less involving to the extent that the subject (viewer or reader) makes fewer connections and personal references between his or her life and the medium's stimuli. Television seems to ask little of viewers in these respects. It presents a flurry of electronic images too rapidly for review or reflection. Consequently, the viewer tends to sit still, eyes fixed on the screen, accepting—without evaluation or criticism—the flickering images. Herbert Krugman, a psychologist interested in consumer advertising research, has elaborated on low-involvement learning.[3] He and his coauthors suggest that images and ideas may be picked up and stored passively. Whereas active, voluntary attention requires constant effort to maintain attention on the stimulus (such as with written material), passive, involuntary attention needs no such effort. A stimulus such as television, with its fast-paced, ever-changing style, short-circuits active attention and holds the viewer's attention in a passive mode in which he has little "aroused resistance to what is learned." The authors compare this learning state to "subliminal perception, extrasensory perception, or hypnotism."[4]

Krugman, the argument continues, makes the right connection by comparing television to hypnotism. Television, according to this argument, prepares viewers to accept its messages in the same way a hypnotist mesmerizes someone. The hypnotist also has the subject sit still and concentrate on a light source (often flickering) in a darkened room. Under such conditions, people often become quite malleable and susceptible to suggestion.

The argument also incorporates discoveries about the specialized functions of the two halves of the human brain. The left half of the brain governs our capacity for logic, reasoning, language, and mathematics, while the right half is concerned with images, art, music, and creative impulses. However, the two halves communicate substantially during most mental processes.

The proponents of this rationale theorize that television viewing requires the right half of the brain to work very hard. The television screen consists of hundreds of rows of tiny fluorescent dots that are illuminated in sequence by an electronic gun that continually races across them. The varying intensity of these illuminations constructs patterns that we see as pictures. However, no picture per se actually exists on the screen at any given time. Instead, the human eye and brain record and store the perceived sequence of illuminated dots, packaging this information to compose the images we see. This task is so demanding that it uses virtually all of the brain's image-processing capacity.

The argument concludes that the television viewer does not, indeed cannot, criticize or evaluate the images and messages he perceives because, while the right half of the brain is completely occupied with composing images from dots, the left half shuts down. Neither criticism nor logical evaluation, both left-brain functions, can occur because the right brain is too busy to communicate with the left.

This lack of intellectual participation while viewing television ultimately deprives viewers of their autonomy. Human brains are ill-equipped to differentiate between artificial television images and their real life counterparts. Consequently, people use television images just as they do data from real life—to formulate attitudes about work, love, sex, friendship, consumer goods, politics, and so forth. These television images, however, were not critiqued when first perceived. Therefore, in a sense, the viewer did not choose to hold them, let alone to embrace the attendant attitudes and preferences. The viewer really decided only whether or not to watch television.

THE EVIDENCE

The available evidence, though sparse, suggests that the foregoing argument is somewhat overstated. First, a set of studies on the sociology of television viewing shows that people look at television screens only about 60 percent of the time they are on.[5] Further, when people watch in groups, they often talk with one another and sometimes become quite excited and animated.[6] Neither of these observations especially supports the version of low-involvement learning that borders on hypnotism, in which the viewer sits, transfixed in darkness, hypnotized by the television screen.

These findings, however, may be consistent with the less extreme version of low-involvement learning from television. Therefore, sufficient learning to alter at least some behavior patterns may be possible without effort or choice from watching television. But this is undoubtedly true of print, also; Krugman contends that magazine ads are also likely to cause low-involvement learning. Therefore, this version of low-involvement learning does not distinguish broadcast from print.

Evidence provides only limited support for the dot-scan/left-right brain portions of the preceding argument. For one thing, virtually all of the research has dealt exclusively with advertising, leaving us to guess what results experiments using more engrossing fare, such as dramas or sporting events, would offer. A more serious problem is that some of the research data does not confirm the hypothesis. For example, in *Brain Activity and Recall of TV Advertising,*[7] the authors recorded the brain-wave patterns of thirty right-handed women who watched television commercials. Using an electroencephalograph, the authors measured the occurrence of alpha waves (electrical currents in the brain with frequencies between eight and twelve cycles per second) in each half of the brain. The presence of alpha waves is considered indicative of a "normal awake but inattentive adult."[8] If viewing television is primarily a right-brain activity, then a viewer's left brain, unengaged as it were, should have more alpha waves. The authors showed their subjects twenty television commercials, with no program material between them, three times each. They found that viewing the commercials produced more alpha waves in the right brain, indicating more left-brain than right-brain activity—the opposite of their working hypothesis.[9]

Herbert Krugman, commenting on this research, attempted to show that the data could support a version of the original hypothesis.[10] He noted that the initial exposure to the commercials produced a level of left-brain activity that declined dramatically with subsequent viewings. By the third viewing, the subjects' right- and left-brain activity had approximately equalized. Krugman postulated that, while television exhausted the left brain's attention, the right brain would not tire of watching. Therefore, he concluded, the time trend away from more left-brain activity supported the hypothesis that television is primarily a right-brain activity.

Krugman's reanalysis actually proves nothing; it only shows a way that the original hypothesis *might* be consistent with the data. Although the experiment showed relatively more right-brain activity during later viewings, the data did not suggest that there was, in absolute terms, more right-brain than left-brain activity. At most, one can speculate that, if viewing had continued beyond the end of the actual experiment, the observed trend might have continued, and ultimately the subjects might have displayed greater right-brain activity. Hence, these data might be consistent with the original hypothesis, but they are too incomplete to be conclusive.

A subsequent article, *Brain-Activity Responses to Magazine and Television Advertising,*[11] reports an experiment in which the authors monitored the brain waves of thirty right-handed women who either watched television commercials or read magazine advertisements. The investigation included an experimental television presentation wherein two sets of four television commercials each were shown during the first twenty-four minutes of "an action-adventure movie," at seven and sixteen minutes after it began.[12] In addition, thirty seconds of blank leader were added before and after the film. As the subjects viewed the presentation, including the inserts, the investigators monitored their brain waves. They also conducted a parallel experiment for print, creating a "magazine" by placing eight double-page advertisements, "11 single page filler ads, and 28 editorial pages" into a spiral binder.[13] Blank pages were inserted at the front and back of the binder. The researchers then monitored the subjects' brain waves as they looked through the binder.

The investigators found that reading generated more intense brain activity in both the left and right halves of the brain than did viewing television. They found little support, however, for the contention that viewing television is more right-brain–dominated than reading.[14] In fact, only one finding supported the hypothesis. The researchers compared the relative levels of left-brain versus right-brain activity when subjects first looked at a blank (but illuminated) television screen, and then looked at the commercials. When the subjects viewed the commercials, their right brains became comparatively more active. When the researchers compared the subjects' left-brain versus right-brain activities as they looked at the blank magazine page, and then at the double-page ads, the *left* brain generated comparatively more activity.

Two serious problems plague this finding, though. First, when the researchers made the same comparison of brain activity with commercials presented first and a blank page or screen, second, no such results appeared. Second, to view this result as confirming the hypothesis, one must presume that the brain's activity while looking at a blank screen or page is the appropriate base line. The authors provide no theoretical justification for such a presumption.

Nothing else in this article supports the basic hypothesis. In fact, the most striking aspect of the findings is the general equality of left- and right-brain activity during both reading and television viewing.[15]

An additional bit of evidence that casts doubt upon the dot-scan portion of the theory is presented by Krugman in his article *Brain Wave Measures of Media Involvement.*[16] Here, Krugman recorded the brain waves of one woman who watched a set of three commercial advertisements, first on a simulated television—"a Fairchild 400 rear projector with an 8 by 11-inch screen"—and then with a real television set. The results were "almost identical."[17] However, the dot-scan portion of the theory might suggest that the real television should produce relatively more right-brain activity.

In contrast to these studies, others have tended to support the hypotheses outlined above. These are collected and summarized in *A Choice of Futures,*[18] and will not be examined here.

All of this experimental work on brain waves is contradictory at best. Further, the basic argument about improper persuasion stumbles on two additional obstacles in the data. First, the connection between recorded brain-wave activity and quality of thinking at that moment is by no means perfect.[19] Second, even if the connection were perfect, it would say nothing of a person's ability to review initial impressions more critically at a later time. Such review may take place after a program is over, but, as the sociological findings indicate, so much of the viewing time is actually spent looking away from the screen or talking that the reviewing process may take place even during the program itself. Together, the inconclusive data and these alternative interpretations of it preclude acceptance of the basic argument. If the theory bears any burden of proof whatsoever—and such a radical argument must bear at least some burden—then the argument fails. Hence, I can find no general difference between persuasion in print and in broadcast that will support differential regulation of content.

5 Sexually Explicit Material and Aggressive Behavior

S OME claim that broadcasting—particularly video—must be regulated to prevent the deterioration of viewers' behavior. I will now examine a rationale for regulation premised on a supposed link between sexually explicit materials[1] and "bad" behavior[2]—primarily sexually aggressive acts, such as rape. One example of such bad behavior produced a lawsuit in 1977. The television film *Born Innocent* contained a scene in which an adolescent girl was "raped" with a "plumber's helper" by four other girls. In *Olivia v. Nat'l Broadcasting Co.,*[3] a nine-year-old girl, who had been raped with a bottle by three children four days after the airing of *Born Innocent,* charged NBC with inciting the brutal act. The California Appellate Court ruled that, despite first amendment protections, the plaintiff was entitled to present before a jury evidence which she contended would prove that the showing of the television drama resulted in actionable injuries.

My threshold question is whether sexually explicit printed material affects people differently from sexually explicit video (or audio) material. An extended review of the literature reveals no systematic differences.

Nothing in the following analysis suggests either that we should make erotica freely available to consenting adults, or that we should tightly control its dissemination. Such conclusions would require complex normative arguments that involve weighing liberty interests against the possible pernicious effects of erotica. I do not attempt to make such arguments in this book, but I do conclude that, however such arguments are resolved with respect to print, they should, in general, be resolved similarly with respect to broadcast.

THEORIES OF SEX AND AGGRESSION

To appreciate fully the experimental and field work data I discuss in this book, it would be helpful to have a complete theory of the relationship between sex and aggression. Unfortunately, no such theory, with specific predictive power, seems to exist. The partial theories on the link between sex and aggression that are found in the literature can be summarized as follows:

Arousal theories

Arousal-frustration. Once sexually aroused, a person seeks sexual gratification. If not soon gratified, he or she becomes frustrated and upset, leading to aggressive behavior.[4]

General arousal. Sexual stimulation produces arousal of a general nature, enhancing aggressive, as well as all other kinds of behavior.[5]

Specific arousal. There is a direct, partly physiological link between sexual arousal and aggressive arousal and triggering one will bring about the other.[6]

Arousal mislabeling. A sexually aroused person undergoes a series of physiological changes (such as accelerated heart-beat rate, increased perspiration, etc.) which he or she then labels, in a sense, as either sexual excitation or anger. If angered soon before or soon after being sexually aroused, he or she may mislabel the sexual arousal as greater anger, which leads to greater aggressiveness.[7]

Modeling theories

General modeling. Viewing sexually aggressive materials (such as rape scenes) will cause men to accept that behavior. Later, almost as a conditioned response, they will engage in such behavior themselves when prompted by certain cues, such as feeling angry with a woman.[8] A very similar version of this theory asserts that men will consciously select this sort of behavior in cued situations.[9]

Disinhibition. Society inhibits naturally aggressive behaviors, such as rape, by its norms and values. Viewing or reading depictions of sexually aggressive behavior, such as rape, might disinhibit men from performing these natural, aggressive acts.[10]

Value/attitude/preference changes. Watching sexually aggressive matter might change the viewers' value systems, causing them to prefer sexual agression.[11]

These theories are far from satisfactory. None can explain all, or even most, of the experimental and empirical data, nor is any one completely independent of the others. They do, however, show something of the suppositions and thought processes of the social psychologists who conducted the experiments described below.

EVIDENCE ON SEX AND AGGRESSION

First I will review experimental work,[12] which takes place in controlled, laboratory settings, and then examine field work, which gathers and interprets data about society at large. The categories of experimental and field work overlap, but are useful for organizing the data.

Experimental Evidence

The experiments I review use different types of subjects, treat them differently, and, in the end, measure different things. The subjects tend to be divided into either groups of women and men or groups of "normals" (defined as people without detected aberrant sexual proclivities) and deviants (such as rapists and pedophiles). Virtually all of the deviants studied are men, and nearly all of the normals studied are college-age adults. These subjects are almost all volunteers. All laboratory and field experiments that depend on volunteers may suffer, to some extent, if volunteers differ significantly from the general population.[13] Because there is no reason to suspect that "volunteer effects" systematically vary by the type of medium employed in the experiment, I will disregard these effects for the purposes of this book.

After introducing general experimental technique in the area, I will discuss the findings first with respect to normals, and then, quite briefly, deviants. I will not discuss whether or not sexually explicit broadcast material produces more bad effects in children than printed matter does, principally because there is virtually no material on this point to review. (The separate questions of differential *accessibility* to children of broadcast and print are reviewed in chapter 7.)

The researchers treated their subjects differently in several important ways. Most significantly for my purposes, they changed the media from experiment to experiment. Print, television, film, radio, slides, and live readings were all employed. Unfortunately, the existing literature essentially ignores possible differences among these media. Therefore to answer the questions I have raised, I will look for general patterns in the results of the print experiments. I will do the same for the work in television and film, and then will compare these patterns. For this comparison I will consolidate television and film into one category, as few of the experimental reports indicate whether the material was presented via projector or on a television screen. This consolidation will probably bolster the case for the regulation of broadcast, because subjects often displayed aggressive behaviors in response to viewing certain films.

Not only did the researchers vary the medium, they also changed the material itself. Subjects were exposed to a broad range of sexually explicit matter, everything from consensual behavior to forced sexual contact which the victim detested to forced sex which the victim ultimately enjoyed. Some researchers added an anger variable, insulting or electronically shocking their subjects, while others did not.

The experiments monitored several different output variables. Most importantly, they tried to measure changes in either physical or verbal aggression. Physical aggression was almost always measured on a "Buss aggression machine," a device that the subject was told would shock another person, that person being a secret confederate of the experimenter. In fact, all the machine did was record the number and intensity of electric shocks that the subject tried to give the confederate. Verbal aggression was tested much less often, and was measured on a scale of aggressiveness. Experimenters also monitored attitude changes, particularly with respect to using force in sexual relations. Lastly, they compared arousal levels in response to various stimuli.

Arousal was measured in three different ways: self-report, physical changes—such as change in penile tumescence or vaginal blood flow—and biochemical changes—such as changes in the level of acid phosphotase in the urine. Recent evidence suggests, however, that men may be able to control their extent of erection so much that penile tumescence is a poor measure of "true" arousal, particularly in rapists.[14]

Experimental evidence on normal subjects—TV and film. According to the current sociological and psychological literature,[15] normal males who view sexually explicit films or television tend to become more aggressive. This is especially true if, during the experiment: (1) their victims are women; (2) the men have been angered; and (3) they have been "disinhibited" from acting aggressively, which means that they have been treated in a way which allows them to feel freer to aggress.[16]

Examining a few recent studies in detail reveals something of the methodology and importance of the modern experimental work. Donnerstein's work, *Aggressive Erotica and Violence Against Women,*[17] involved exposing male undergraduates to the following procedure. Males played both the experimenter and his assistant. A confederate of the experimenter, posing as another subject, was played half the time by a male, and the other half by a female. The experimenter first introduced the true subject to the confederate and told the subject that the confederate was a subject. The confederate and subject then listened to prerecorded instructions explaining that the experiment concerned the effects of stress on both learning and physiological activities. (The experimenter monitored the subjects' blood pressure at various times during the experiment.) The instructions also said that electric shocks would be administered during the experiment.

Next, the experimenter "selected" the confederate to go to another room. He then directed the subject to a second room, immediately adjacent to the confederate's, and asked the subject to assist him by writing a five minute essay on a given topic. The essay was to be read and evaluated by the confederate, who would signal his or her evaluation by administering shocks to the subject—no shocks for the best evaluation to ten shocks for the worst. When the experimenter returned, he took the subject's essay to the confederate for "evaluation," and then put electrodes on the subject's fingers. The subject was given either one shock (no anger condition) or nine shocks (anger condition). In addition, the experimenter gave the subject a written evaluation of the essay, which was either complimentary (no anger condition) or quite derogatory (anger condition).

The experimenter then removed the subject's electrodes and asked him to view a short motion picture intended for use in future research. All subjects agreed and were shown one of three films: (1) a talk show interview (neutral condition); (2) a depiction of a young couple engaging in sexual intercourse (erotic condition); or (3) a depiction of a man with a gun forcing his way into the home of a woman and forcing her to have sexual intercourse with him (aggressive erotic condition). After viewing the film, each subject was asked to evaluate the confederate's performance on a test involving memorization of nonsense syllables that he or she had supposedly taken. As before, evaluations consisted of electric shocks, but this time the tables were turned. Additionally, the experimenter always marked two-thirds of the test answers "incorrect."[18]

Donnerstein's results show that "for subjects paired with a male target, both the erotic and aggressive-erotic films increased aggression" by approximately the same amount when compared to the neutral film, but that with a *female* target, only the aggressive-erotic film produced greater aggression. Donnerstein offers two different theories to explain the failure of nonaggressive erotica to produce higher aggression levels when subjects had female targets. For nonangered subjects, he hypothesizes that they could have regarded their arousal as merely sexual desire. For angered subjects, whom he expects would have labeled increased arousal as anger, he hypothesizes that societal inhibitions may have blocked aggressive activity against females.

Donnerstein explains the elicitation of greatly increased aggression against female targets from viewing aggressive erotica by theorizing that subjects associate the female victim in the film with the female target. He produces no more detailed theory of how the association leads to greater aggression.

Donnerstein's experiment yields insights about the interaction of anger and the type of film viewed. Note that the experiment has a $2 \times 2 \times 3$ factorial design, measuring the relationships between anger (anger, no anger), sex of target (male, female), and films (neutral, erotic, and aggressive erotic). This design enabled Donnerstein to compare the effects on male aggression of the three types of films (measured by the number of shocks delivered), while also accounting for the subject's anger and the target's gender as variables. When he analyzed the correlation between anger and the type of film viewed, he found that, while in general films do not produce much change in viewers' behavior, they do produce substantial effects on angered viewers. Donnerstein found an additional disturbing result: "even when individuals were not angered, the aggressive-erotic film did increase aggression against the female target."[19]

This work represents an advance over the earlier work, such as Donnerstein and Barrett, *Effects of Erotic Stimuli on Male Aggression Toward Females,*[20] in which the authors used a research design identical to the one described, except that only two types of films (neutral and nonaggressive erotic) were used. Donnerstein and Barrett found that the erotic films increased aggressiveness against males when compared to the neutral film, but that aggression was probably inhibited for subjects who were paired with a female target. These results are completely consistent with later work, but provide a misleading picture of the possible social effects of sexually explicit matter because they fail to consider the nature of the stories told in the sexually explicit films.

An experiment reported in Donnerstein and Hallam's *Facilitating Effects of Erotica on Aggression Against Women*[21] used the research design described above, with the following exceptions. First, two types of films were shown: violent but nonsexual selections from *The Wild Bunch* (aggressive condition), and "'stag' films depicting various forms of sexual intercourse (oral, anal) in addition to female homosexuality"[22] (erotic condition). Rather than a neutral film, a third group of subjects was shown no film at all (no film condition). Next, all subjects were angered (in that they were treated to nine electric shocks and derogatory evaluations of their essays). Last, each subject was allowed to "shock" the confederate during two separate evaluations of the confederate's work, immediately after watching the film, and then again ten minutes later. In the "no-film" condition, subjects sat and waited for a period of time equal to the length of the film before first being allowed to shock the confederate.

The results showed that viewers of the violent film displayed more aggression toward male than toward female targets, during both evaluations, and more aggression toward targets of either sex than did subjects who saw no film at all. The erotic film produced quite different results. Immediately after seeing it, viewers registered only slightly more aggression toward all targets than did subjects who saw no film. Most significantly, however, when these subjects were given a second chance to aggress, they gave many more shocks to female, but not male, targets.

The authors offer several possible explanations for this phenomenon. The best is that a first opportunity to aggress disinhibits further aggression. Their alternative hypotheses are: (1) an individual's previous aggression may give him "a source of aggressive cues" for subsequent aggression; (2) previous aggression may reinforce later aggression, either by reducing the aggressor's tension or by giving him knowledge that the victim has suffered; or (3) some subjects may want to appear consistent in the two aggression opportunities. These attempts to explain why the erotica increased aggression against only female targets suggest both the lack of a comprehensive, coherent theory relating sex and aggression, and possible methodological flaws in the experiment. The authors say they chose the erotic films with no "aggressive content in mind,"[23] but worry that films might contain some "process" of "implied aggression"[24] against females. Whatever this "process" is, it undoubtedly has a place in a comprehensive theory of sex and aggression. Until such a theory is developed, however, I would suggest that Donnerstein and Hallam reconsider the wisdom of using films including anal intercourse as nonaggressive erotica.[25]

Earlier, similar work by Dolf Zillmann and associates shows that exposing previously angered subjects to erotic films can dramatically increase the subjects' aggression levels.[26] Zillmann used a film of "a young couple engaging in sexual foreplay and performing face to face intercourse in various positions. Their behavior was devoid of indications of wild passion which could have been interpreted as aggressive."[27] Zillmann believes the results support the "excitation-transfer" model, a two-stage model in which a subject first decides he is angry and then, by appraising the extent of his physiological arousal, determines just how angry he is. The more aroused he is, the angrier he will consider himself to be, regardless of what initially sparked his arousal.

Mueller and Donnerstein's *Film Facilitated Arousal and Pro Social Behavior*[28] supports an excitation transfer model for prosocial behavior, as opposed to aggression. Subjects were allowed to reward rather than punish the experimenter's confederate. Subjects who had been treated in a positive manner and had seen an arousing film gave the confederate better rewards. Reward behavior was lower for subjects who had been negatively or neutrally treated, or who had seen neutral films.

A few experiments attempt to gauge the long-range effects of exposure to pornography. An early work by Reifler, Howard, Lipton, Liptzin, and Widmann, *Pornography: An Experimental Study of Effects,*[29] measured long-range effects on *arousal* from exposure to pornography by exposing twenty-three males to pornography in all forms of media for ninety minutes every day for three weeks. The subjects' arousal fell substantially over the three-week period. These subjects were shown the same materials every day throughout the period, plus additional material during the third week. Therefore, the subjects may have been bored by seeing the same material over and over. However, in a more recent study experimenters exposed subjects to massive amounts of different erotic films over a period of six weeks, but interest and arousal still faded significantly. Eight weeks later subjects reexposed to pornography showed some recovery from the previous loss in responsiveness. The authors question the significance of the boredom phenomenon for nonexperimental situations, claiming that the standard situation for most people is occasional exposure, which may in fact "foster increased liking of erotica rather than boredom."[30]

One of the most intriguing of the recent field experiments tested the long-term impact of various films on male and female subjects' attitudes concerning violence against women.[31] Neil Malamuth and V. P. Check divided a large group of undergraduate students into three groups: (1) those who saw no movie (control untreated); (2) those who viewed *A Man and A Woman* and *Hooper,* both full-length movies that "excluded all forms of sexual violence"[32] (control exposure); and (3) those who viewed *Swept Away* and *The Getaway,* two full-length movies featuring explicit scenes of women being raped and eventually enjoying the experience (experimental exposure). All subjects in the last two groups saw one picture each at two different theaters, a commercial one off campus and another on campus, making this a field, rather than laboratory experiment.

Several days later, the experimenters gave the subjects an "Attitudes Survey," containing questions based on an "Acceptance of Interpersonal Violence (AIV)" scale and a "Rape Myth Acceptance (RMA)" scale. The questions asked the extent of the subjects' agreement[33] with a series of statements such as, "'A man is never justified in hitting his wife' (AIV scale)"[34] and "'Many women have an unconscious wish to be raped and may then unconsciously set up a situation in which they are likely to be attacked' (RMA scale)."[35] This last statement is a typical example of a rape myth.

To digress for a moment, rape myths are a set of false, prejudicial beliefs about rape which are widely held in our society, and which generally shift moral blame for a rape from the rapist to the victim.[36] Certain feminists and sociologists have attacked the mass media for creating messages that perpetuate rape myths, thus creating an environment that is hostile to rape victims.

Empirical studies have attempted to find factors that might predict rape myth acceptance. Martha Burt has shown that acceptance of interpersonal violence is the strongest predictor of RMA. Other predictors include sexual conservatism, sex role stereotypes, and adversarial sexual beliefs (the belief that sexual relationships are always exploitative).[37]

Burt tested several additional variables, one of which was "media exposure to depictions of sexual assault." The media included newspapers, TV, movies, and so forth. Media exposure was treated as an experimental variable, as opposed to variables on attitude, personality, and background of subjects. Of the four types of variables, exposure had the least consistent and least important effect on rape myth acceptance and was found to lower RMA for men, but not for women.

Malamuth and Check's results show that the experimental exposure treatment (*Swept Away* and *The Getaway*) produced a substantial increase in the AIV score and a slight increase on the RMA scale for males. Females showed a slight decrease on both scales. The authors present two different hypotheses to explain their results. One theory concerns "attitude polarization." This suggests that men and women focus on aspects of the films that confirm their differing preconceptions. Male preconceptions are much more accepting of both violence against women and rape myths than are female preconceptions. Therefore, the films produce an increase on the RMA and AIV scales for men, who concentrate on the female victims' ultimate enjoyment, and a decrease on the scales for women, who concentrate on the female victims' expressions of pain. However, the authors are skeptical that there are enough data in the films to support the "attitude polarization" hypothesis for female subjects. They offer instead a "reactance" theory—that females, upon seeing such films, react by considering why the message they have seen must be false. A problem with this theory is that it does not explain the results for male subjects.

Dolf Zillmann and Jennings Bryant[38] also tested changes in subjects' beliefs and attitudes after viewing erotic films. These films, however, contained no depictions of force or pain. Massive exposure to this material resulted in: (1) loss of compassion toward women as rape victims, and toward women in general; (2) increases in subjects' estimates of numbers of adults practicing common and uncommon sexual behaviors such as oral sex, anal intercourse, group sex, sadomasochism, and bestiality (subjects with massive exposure tended more accurately to estimate "common" sexual behaviors—for example, oral sex—but tended to overestimate less common behaviors—for example, bestiality); (3) decreased evaluation of explicit erotic films as "offensive" or "pornographic"; and (4) fewer recommendations that explicit sexual films be restricted to minors or regulated in any other way.

Edward Donnerstein and Leonard Berkowitz have proposed a theory about male subjects that could help explain these results.[39] They found that angered and nonangered male subjects increased their aggression after viewing aggressive-erotic films that depicted women as ultimately enjoying rape. They theorize such "positive" endings may disinhibit male aggressiveness by implying not so subtly that aggression is justified. Additionally, the authors found that angered subjects who viewed films depicting women who did not enjoy being raped also registered increased aggressiveness. The authors believe that angry men want to inflict injury and that, especially for men who are angry at women, seeing a woman in pain gives them "pain cues" that facilitate aggression.[40]

I believe we can conclude from the evidence I have presented that men who watch sexually explicit matter tend to become more aggressive,[41] especially if: (1) their targets of aggression are women; (2) they have been angered or insulted; or (3) they have been disinhibited from acting aggressively. Males may become disinhibited by having more than one chance to aggress against a female target, or by viewing a film whose message is that females enjoy being targets.[42]

Experimental evidence on normal subjects—print evidence. No studies to date have tried to hold erotic content constant while systematically testing for the effects of different media. The literature on sexually explicit printed materials, however, presents findings very similar to those obtained from television and film studies. The only differences suggest that print may be slightly more potent than video, as sexually explicit print material may increase aggression regardless of whether or not subjects are angered, and regardless of whether or not they are disinhibited from aggression against women. I discuss the implications of these differences later.

Edward Donnerstein and associates[43] found that increased aggression in angered subjects may depend on whether subjects were angered before or after viewing erotic magazine photos. When subjects were angered before looking at mildly erotic pictures, subsequent aggression levels were lower. Therefore erotica may have distracted and subdued them. When subjects were angered before looking at highly erotic pictures, subsequent aggression levels were very similar to those in neutral nonangered conditions. Thus anger may have been dissipated by the photos.

In contrast, when subjects were angered after viewing photos, aggression levels increased somewhat for viewers of mild erotica and significantly for viewers of highly erotic pictures. The authors' explanation is that the arousal from highly erotic photos was interpreted as anger by the subjects, thus facilitating aggression. Because this phenomenon of mislabeling arousal has also been found for film, the experimental evidence may show similar effects for television/film and for print, at least for highly explicit erotica.[44]

A more recent study has found that severely provoked persons are not calmed down by mild erotica (slides of *Playboy* models), and therefore do not exhibit the reduction in aggressiveness seen in mildly provoked subjects. Nevertheless, the authors feel that exposure to mild erotica can probably soothe the mild annoyances of everyday life.[45]

In another study, Malamuth and associates[46] gave male and female undergraduates one of eight different rape stories to read, after which they measured the students' sexual arousal. The stories were produced by fully crossing three variables: pain, intent, and outcome. For the pain variable, one version of the story (pain) referred repeatedly to "the woman's experiencing *waves of pain, discomfort, hurting, soreness,* and *aching,*"[47] while another version (no pain) made no such references. For the intent variable, one version (premeditated) referred to the rapist's having planned the assault for days, whereas another version (unplanned) described the rapist as involuntarily losing self control. For the outcome variable, one version (nausea) concluded "Mary Ann found herself overcome with disgust, which sent her reeling into a state of extreme nausea," while another version (orgasm) ended: "Mary Ann found herself overcome with passion, which sent her reeling into a violent orgasm."[48]

The authors found that, for females, the no-pain/orgasm story produced much greater arousal than the no-pain/nausea version, but that when the victim did experience pain, moving from nausea to orgasm produced no significant increase in arousal. For males, the pain/orgasm story produced much greater sexual arousal than the pain/nausea story, but the no-pain story elicited no such difference. The authors think the orgasm version may disinhibit arousal by "minimizing guilt feelings," allowing subjects to "reinterpret the events preceding the argasm so as to believe that consent had been given."[49]

The authors explain the pain effect for males either as a misunderstanding or "mislabelling" of the pain terms as pleasure terms, or as a manifestation of "power." Again, the lack of a comprehensive theory of sex and aggression produces such ad hoc explanations.

A very similar study by Malamuth and Check tested nearly the same variables.[50] Subjects, both male and female, read one of eight erotic passages, which crossed consent, pain, and outcome. Thus the only difference between this study and the one by Malamuth, Heim, and Feshback was that *consent* (of the woman) was substituted for *intent* (of the man) as a variable. The outcome dimension was the only variable that significantly affected subjects' arousal. When the outcome for the woman was positive, subjects were more aroused, irrespective of whether the woman had consented. Malamuth and Check's explanation for this result is that sex role socialization has taught us that women hide their sexual interests. Therefore, subjects focused on the woman's perceived sexual responses rather than other factors. If a woman is disgusted, arousal is decreased, regardless of indications that she consented. More importantly, indications that she is aroused (positive outcome) may create a context in which other potential inhibitors (lack of consent, pain, violence) have no effect.

In Malamuth and Check, *Penile Tumescence and Perceptual Responses to Rape as a Function of Victim's Perceived Reactions*,[51] the outcome was also the main determinant of arousal. Subjects listened to audio tapes of erotic stories that crossed consent and outcome. Male subjects were more aroused by rape stories with a positive outcome for the woman than by rape stories that depicted the woman's abhorrence of the experience. Additionally, subjects' previous exposure to a negative outcome version inhibited their sexual responsiveness to a "neutral" outcome rape story. These findings correlate well with other print studies.

Yoram Jaffe and coauthors[52] measured the increase in subjects' willingness to inflict pain after reading sexually explicit matter. Each male or female subject read a passage, which was either a science fiction story "devoid of erotic and also of aggressive content"[53] (control condition), or three short erotic stories (erotic condition). Unfortunately, the authors give no hint as to the mix of consensual and nonconsensual sexual activity described in the erotic passages, a variable that other studies suggest may be very important. After reading the material, the subjects were allowed to administer shocks to an experimental confederate, who was either male or female, whenever the confederate gave incorrect answers during a bogus extrasensory perception experiment. There was no direct angering procedure in this experiment, although the subjects were each given two mild shocks, ostensibly to acquaint them with the nature of the shocks to be administered to the confederate. Unfortunately, because of the experimental design, one cannot differentiate between subjects' aggressiveness and their desire to aid the confederate's ESP. In any event, the results showed that the erotic material prompted much greater levels of administered shocks to the confederate, and that both males and females who were sexually aroused tended to administer more intense shocks than did nonaroused subjects.

This finding contradicted the findings of earlier works, as well as some more recent works I have already discussed, in that this experiment incorporated no explicit disinhibiting mechanism for males shocking females.

In Malamuth, Haber and Feshbach, *Testing Hypotheses Regarding Rape: Exposure to Sexual Violence, Sex Differences, and the "Normality" of Rapists,*[54] male and female subjects read either a sadomasochistic erotic story (in which a woman experiences intense sexual arousal when a man inflicts pain upon her) or a nonviolent erotic story. Then all subjects read a rape story, in which the victim is "continuously portrayed as clearly opposing the assault."[55] Unlike all other subjects, males who had read the sadomasochistic erotic story were more aroused by the subsequent rape story if they perceived the story's rape victim as experiencing greater pain.

There is additional work which suggests that erotica, in printed form, may inhibit, rather than elicit, aggression. For example, Robert A. Baron, in *The Aggression-Inhibiting Influence of Heightened Sexual Arousal,*[56] indicates that viewing still photographs of "extremely attractive, nude young women" caused previously angered male subjects to reduce their aggression. Social psychologists explain such results as the product of mildly arousing erotica (for example, still nudes) as opposed to highly arousing erotica (for example, written or filmed depictions of sexual intercourse).[57]

Baron and Paul Bell[58] tested angered subjects' aggression after the subjects were exposed to one of five types of print media. Subjects either looked at pictures of scenery (control group), semi-nude females, nude females, or couples making love, or read explicit, erotic stories. Exposure to milder erotic stimuli inhibited later aggression, while exposure to the more arousing sexual materials neither facilitated nor inhibited later aggression. Thus, the findings differed from those in similar experiments with television and film.[59] Baron and Bell suggest that even the erotic passages, the most arousing stimuli employed in their study, were not sufficiently arousing to increase aggression. They used print media for uniformity with Jaffe, who had found subjects' aggression increased after subjects read erotic passages.[60] However, Jaffe's passages, as noted by Baron and Bell, were longer and more explicit. Baron and Bell suggest that films of actual lovemaking might facilitate aggression where the erotic stories did not. They base this suggesion on their intuition that films produce more impact than print.[61]

Experimental evidence on deviants—all media. Fewer experiments, in any medium, have tested the effects of sexually explicit material on convicted sex offenders rather than on normal adults. The work that has been done, however, suggests no great difference between any of the media.[62]

I refer to convicted sex offenders because recent work has suggested that a very large percentage of the male subjects included within the "normal" class may also have a strong propensity to rape.[63] Several studies have asked "normal" male college students to assess the probability on a scale from 1 (not at all likely) to 5 (very likely) that they would rape if they were certain they would not be caught (termed their "LR" report); an overall 35 percent responded 2 or above, and 20 percent indicated 3 or above.[64] Such LR data may be very meaningful, because high LR correlates closely with other factors found to characterize rapists. In contrast to low-LR subjects, high-LR college males and convicted rapists both tend to believe rape myths, discussed above, and experience substantial sexual arousal in response to depictions of rape. Low-LR subjects tend to experience much less sexual arousal and tend not to believe the myths. Belief in rape myths may be very significant, because Malamuth[65] provides evidence that men who believe in rape myths are much more willing, at least in laboratory settings, to aggress against women.

Convicted rapists experience equally high levels of sexual

arousal in response to portrayals of mutually consenting sexual acts or rape. Low-LR "normal" men generally do not become aroused in response to depictions of rape in which the victim is portrayed as abhorring the experience, but experience high levels of arousal with depictions of mutually consenting sex. High-LR males' arousal patterns closely resemble those of convicted rapists. In sum, there are some good reasons for believing a man who says he would rape if given the chance. Among the "normal" population there are many such men.

Field Evidence

Available field evidence clusters into two categories. One group investigates the correlation between the availability of sexually explicit matter and rates of antisocial behavior, particularly rape and other sexual offenses. Unfortunately, this work fails to consider the availability of each medium of pornography separately,[66] and hence provides no useful data for this book. In addition, these studies, as a group, tell very little about the existence of a link between pornography and antisocial acts.

First, it is virtually impossible to measure accurately either the availability of sexually explicit matter or the rates of antisocial behavior.[67] Availability is difficult to measure because of difficulties in defining and categorizing the materials to be studied, and because people pass such materials between themselves without leaving any record. The nature of available material may also change. For example, Neil M. Malamuth and Barry Spinner, in *Longitudinal Content Analysis of Sexual Violence in the Best-Selling Erotic Magazines,*[68] evaluated the content of *Playboy* and *Penthouse* pictures and cartoons from 1973 to 1977 and found a clear and consistent increase in sexual violence over that five-year period. They found sexual violence in about 5 percent of the pictorials and 10 percent of the cartoons.

Rates of antisocial acts are also difficult to measure because of the difference between rates of acting and rates of reporting. The act/report difference, and changes in it, can be produced by, among other things, changes in victims' willingness to report such behavior for fear of suffering humiliation, embarrassment, or just loss of valued time, changes in the population's conception of what constitutes improper sexual behavior, or changes in either the law of sex crimes, such as the legalization of all sexual behavior between consenting adults in private in California, or the willingness of police to accept reports of such acts.[69]

Second, to the extent such data are measurable, the studies reach widely varying conclusions.[70] Third, to the extent that a correlation can be shown, it does not prove causation, for some third factor, such as general social attitudes toward sex, might cause the correlation. For example, climatic trends might even add to observed trends in sex-crime rates; rape and sexual assault rates tend to rise dramatically during the summer.[71]

A second group of studies, using interviews, attempts to determine whether convicted sex offenders have substantially abnormal experiences with pornography. Most of these studies also fail to distinguish between the various media, and the few that do show virtually no differences between them.

Michael Goldstein, Harold Kant, Lewis Judd, Clinton Rice and Richard Green, in *Exposure to Pornography and Sexual Behavior in Deviant and Normal Groups,*[72] report that deviants and normals were asked about both their adolescent and recent experiences with pornography in different media. They present raw data in an appendix, and although they present no statistical tests of the differences among the media, a perusal of the data presents a very clear conclusion: across all media (including books and motion pictures), rapists and pedophiles have no more than average exposure to pornography.[73]

Weldon Johnson, Lenore Kupperstein and Joseph Peters, in *Sex Offenders' Experience with Erotica,*[74] report a survey of forty-seven convicted sex offenders and a matched set of normals. The questions, some of which were divided by medium, elicited responses suggesting a minor difference. Sex offenders were more likely to report books as recent sources of pornography, while nonoffenders were more likely to report magazines. In other respects, the different media elicited virtually identical responses.[75]

There is a strong intuition that film is more arousing than print, but no one has properly tested this hypothesis. In general, researchers have often used films of intercourse and related activities as "arousing, explicit sexual material" and photographs of nude women as mild erotica, or "suggestive but comparatively nonarousing fare." They need not do so. Photographs and stories about the same explicitly erotic acts depicted in films or television could be used. A study employing such graphic printed material could test for the differential effects of the two media. However, until such work is done, one must evaluate the existing evidence on the effects of pornography.

Where should we place the burden of proof? There are two obvious alternatives. One alternative is to place the burden of proof on supporters of differential regulation of the media because a bifurcated system probably costs more than a single system. Two different systems of content control for broadcast and print require judges, lawyers, legislators, and litigants to know and understand two different sets of rules, which, all other things being equal, is more expensive than learning just one set. Also, one might believe that citizens benefit psychologically from living in a simpler environment. With two different systems of control, learning to interpret broadcast and print communications becomes more complex. Because television watching, reading, and radio listening comprise a significant portion of human activity, this complexity produces real costs. In sum, because a bifurcated system of content control costs more than a single system, the burden should be on those who would further differential control.

Alternatively, one might assign the burden of proof to those who support change, because there are costs associated with any change, including changing the current institutions of content control in the media. Empirical propositions support the justifications for current institutions; many believe that print and broadcast produce different effects. Those who would disprove the empirical propositions that justify our institutions—in this case those who would prove equality between the media—should bear the burden.

The evidence sustains the second of these burdens of proof but not the first. If there is any presumption that printed and video pornography produce similar effects, the evidence proves that there is no substantial justification for regulating the media differently. Experimental evidence on normal subjects suggests that, of the two, print may be slightly more pernicious, and the evidence on deviant subjects, as well as field evidence, contributes nothing. Such evidence is too weak to disturb a presumption of equality.

Alternatively, many people suspect that video/film erotica is more pernicious than printed erotica. Utilizing a slight presumption that this is true and placing the burden of proof on those claiming equality, the slight evidence that print is more pernicious than video/film sustains the burden of proof. Only if there were some presumption that print is more dangerous than video—which no one seems to believe—would the evidence possibly support differential regulation, with print treated more restrictively. Therefore, the evidence regarding bad effects of sexually explicit materials on adults cannot justify differential regulation of print and broadcast.

6   Children and Violence

MOST social psychological work about television done in the last fifteen years has concentrated on the possibility that viewing violent television programming causes violent or aggressive behavior, usually by children. The possible existence of this causal link, termed the "violence hypothesis,"[1] has helped provoke three sets of congressional hearings[2] and continues to provoke substantial controversy.[3] The violence hypothesis' high political salience derives from a widespread belief that producing hostile, aggressive people harms both society and the hostile individuals.[4] I will not quarrel with this belief despite the plethora of assertiveness training books and classes that might suggest that the issue is controversial. Instead, I will assume that aggressive, violent people are bad, and ask two questions. First, does the existing literature support the violence hypothesis for television differently than it supports the violence hypothesis for print? Second, assuming a difference between the two media exists, what forms of differential regulation would appropriately deal with it?

I will not offer a complete review of the television violence hypothesis. Many recent reviews on this subject already exist[5] and such an excursion here would be far too lengthy. Instead, I will describe some of the original research in order to acquaint the reader with the standard research techniques, and then summarize the general pattern of results. The research material on the violence hypothesis for print media will be reviewed in greater detail, because that literature has not been reviewed recently.

No one disputes that people, particularly children, may learn from television. We can also assume that people who are so inclined can learn violent, criminal acts from television. Indeed, there are a few well-known examples of "copy-cat" crimes resulting from television shows. These include the "Doomsday Flight" program, scripted by Rod Serling, in which a blackmailer claims to have placed an altitude bomb (which detonates automatically if air pressure rises beyond some point) on an airplane and demands a ransom in exchange for divulging the bomb's location. Within one week following the broadcast of "Doomsday Flight," at least thirteen similar threats were received by airlines.[6] (The question of how well people can learn from broadcast, as opposed to print media, is beyond the scope of this book.) I am interested, rather, in any change in the proclivity to engage in antisocial behavior after viewing (or reading) violent fare.

LABORATORY EXPERIMENTAL WORK

Just as with sexually explicit matter, no controlled laboratory experiments have been performed to test the effects of different media.[7] Instead, watching violent television has been compared with watching nonviolent fare, or with doing nothing at all.[8] But no one has compared watching violent television to reading violent matter. After reviewing the vast literature on the effects of television violence, I will compare the general pattern of findings with the results of the few experiments that have tested for the effects of reading violent fare.

All of the work reported is anchored, one way or another, in some theory of the violence hypothesis. These theories all parallel, quite closely, the theories of sex and aggression.

Briefly, these theories are:

Catharsis. Watching or reading about violence satisfies children's taste for indulging in it, thereby leading to a net reduction in violent acts.[9]

Disinhibition. By watching or reading about violent acts in nonthreatening surroundings, children learn to be less anxious and more comfortable with the idea of engaging in the portrayed behaviors, thereby reducing the effectiveness of society's sanctions that are supposed to inhibit bad behavior.[10]

Social Learning. Children learn appropriate social behaviors through imitating models, usually adults. Television and other media offer children adult models who kill, rape, rob, and so forth, which ultimately produces people who think such behaviors are socially appropriate.[11]

Tastes and Preferences. Violent fare acts just like advertisements for criminal activities; children grow up thinking that violence and aggression are fun.[12]

Conditioning. Television and other media repeatedly show children that the best methods of problem solving involve the use of force. When confronted with a problem in real life that closely resembles those vicariously encountered on television, the children automatically respond with force.[13]

Television/Film Experiments

Albert Bandura has produced the most important experimental work on the television violence hypothesis.[14] His work, anchored in "social learning theory," tests the hypothesis that children who see role models engage in aggressive and violent behavior will behave similarly. To test this hypothesis, along with various refinements thereon, Bandura and his associates conducted many experiments. Virtually all of them involved exposing an experimental subgroup to a live, filmed, or cartoon depiction of violent, aggressive behavior, exposing a control group to a nonviolent portrayal or no portrayal at all, and then observing the children's behavior and rating each group for aggression and violence.

In one such study, Albert Bandura, Dorothea Ross, and Sheila A. Ross[15] divided ninety-six nursery school children into four groups: real-life aggression condition; human film aggression condition; cartoon film aggression condition; and control condition. The children in the real-life aggression condition were placed, one at a time, in a room with an adult and a Bobo doll. (A Bobo doll is an inflated plastic form of a clown that is weighted at the bottom so it rights itself automatically if it is pushed over.) The adult first punched the Bobo doll, then sat on it and repeatedly punched it in the face, then lifted the doll and "pummelled it on the head with a mallet," and finally threw the doll in the air and kicked it, all the time saying "Sock him in the nose," "Hit him down," "Kick him," and "Pow." The adult then twice repeated this series of acts.[16] The children in the human film aggression condition saw a film of the same adult performing the exact same aggressive behavior. The children in the cartoon film aggression condition saw a film projected onto a glass lens screen in a television set (so as to simulate a television program) of a woman dressed as a black cat "similar to the many cartoon cats."[17] The set, adorned with artificial grass, brightly colored trees, birds, and butterflies, contained a Bobo doll, which the woman-cat also treated in exactly the same manner.

All of the children were individually escorted to a test room located in a different building, where no other children were present. This room contained a "3-foot Bobo doll, a mallet, a peg board, two dart guns, and a tether ball with a face painted on it"[18] hanging from the ceiling. Observers watched each child for twenty minutes through a one-way mirror, and counted the number of five-second intervals during which the child demonstrated an "aggression." Aggressions included imitating any of the model's aggressive acts or statements; striking anything with a mallet; sitting on the Bobo doll; punching, slapping or pushing any object in the room; hostile remarks, such as "Shoot the Bobo" or "Stupid ball"; or using the dart gun either by firing darts or by aiming the gun at objects and firing imaginary shots.[19]

The researchers compared the average number of aggressive acts per child across each of the four conditions. They found that none of the three noncontrol conditions differed in result, each producing a significantly greater number of aggressive acts than were found in the control group.[20]

A tremendous volume of laboratory research, with slight variations in experimental design, has replicated these results. Some experiments have varied the type of aggressive behavior monitored. A number have replicated the results found by Bandura, Ross, and Ross with children playing together with toys.[21] Other studies have replaced the Bobo doll with a person dressed in a clown suit.[22] Many children who had seen the experimental films attacked the human clown, but very few of the control group children, who saw no films, did so.[23]

Experimenters in this area have also used the Buss aggression machine, described in chapter 5.[24] Although most of these studies used adolescents or college students as subjects,[25] at least two used aggression machine techniques with children. R. M. Liebert and R. A. Baron divided 136 children, five to nine years old, into two groups. The experimental group saw film clips from "The Untouchables,"[26] which included a chase, two fistfights, two shootings, and a knifing.[27] The control group saw clips from exciting sporting events. Later, each child was taken to another room, seated before a Buss aggression machine that had been altered so as to have only "HELP" and "HURT" buttons, and then told that a child in another room was going to play a game that involved turning a handle. The experimenter explained that if the subject pushed the "HELP" button, the handle would be easier to turn, but if the "HURT" button was depressed, the handle would become hot to the touch. The child subject was required to push one of the two buttons every time a white light went on, which the subject was told indicated that the other child had started to turn the handle. Liebert and Baron found that children in the experimental group pushed the "HURT" button significantly more often than did the children in the control group. In a similar experiment using delinquent adolescent boys, Hartmann produced similar results.[28]

Researchers have found analogous results when monitoring verbal "aggression."[29] They have also found that children remember and replicate the aggressive acts over time spans of at least four to six months.[30]

Experimenters have also varied the stimulus used to provoke the aggression. The Bandura, Ross, and Ross experiment described above compared live models to films of live models and to a cartoon model. Other experiments used genuine animated cartoons as a stimulus and produced comparable increases in aggression.[31] In addition, Leonard Berkowitz and Russell Geen's experiments on college students suggest that specific cues in the filmed material may increase aggression.[32] These experiments were conducted by a research assistant, introduced as either Bob or Kirk Anderson, and involved showing an extremely violent fight scene from the motion picture *Champion*, starring Kirk Douglas, to one half of the subjects. The other half of the subjects were shown a film of a nonviolent track meet. Then the subjects, who earlier had been angered by the research assistant, were permitted to shock him using a Buss machine. Those subjects who had seen *Champion* and who were introduced to Kirk Anderson administered more shocks than any other subjects.

Experimenters have also investigated the effects social sanctions have on eliciting aggression. The most obvious question asks whether prohibiting or rewarding aggression affects behavior. Bandura conducted an experiment in which all subjects saw a film of an adult attacking a Bobo doll[33] in the same manner as in the Bandura, Ross, and Ross experiment.[34] The subjects were divided into three groups. One group saw only the basic film. Another saw an additional film of a second adult rewarding the aggressor with a large glass of 7-Up, chocolate bars, Cracker Jack popcorn, and "an assortment of candies," and praising him as a "strong champion." The third group saw, instead, an additional film of a second adult telling the aggressor, "'You quit picking on that clown. I won't tolerate it,'" spanking him with a rolled-up magazine, and then finally warning him, "'If I catch you doing that again, you big bully, I'll give you a hard spanking. You quit acting that way.'"[35] The subjects who saw this last film subsequently exhibited far less aggression than did the subjects in either of the other two groups. However, when an adult entered the play room and offered the children "treats" for aggression similar to the model's acts, many previously unaggressive children began to act aggressively.

Finally, a number of studies have concluded that justifying portrayed violence, by suggesting social approval and utility, tends to increase subsequent aggression in college-age subjects.[36] Five- to six-year-old children, who are so young that they have difficulty understanding the motives of the characters in the programs, do not respond to the justifications.[37]

Print Experiments

The few laboratory experiments that tested the effects of reading violent material on subsequent aggression produced
mixed results. In addition, the reading studies on children
used different methods than the television studies. Where television studies often observed behavior, print studies only surveyed verbal or written responses.

One experiment by Alexis Tan and Kermit Scruggs dis-
covered absolutely no correlation between reading violent material and bad behavior.[38] They divided ninety-five fifth and
sixth graders into two groups. The experimental group read
Daredevils, a violent comic book, while the control group read
Betty and Veronica, a nonviolent comic book. After reading the
comic books, the children answered two sets of questions: one
tested how much of the comic book each child remembered
and another tested how each child would act in various situations. These situations involved real-life problems and were
followed by pairs of possible responses. Each child was told to
choose the response that would more likely mirror his conduct
if confronted with such a situation.

To illustrate, the accompanying cartoons on page 100 por-
tray some of the problems presented to the children.[39] Possible
responses were categorized as either physical violence, verbal
violence, nonviolence, or avoidance of conflict. Subjects' responses were then tallied to measure levels of aggression. No
significant differences between the experimental and control
groups were found. Thus, reading the violent comic book produced no adverse effects.[40]

In contrast, an experiment by Ross D. Parke, Stephen G.
West, and Leonard Berkowitz found that third, fourth, and fifth
graders responded more aggressively after reading violent material.[41] The subject children read either *Adventures of the
Green Berets,* a war comic book, or *Gidget,* a nonaggressive
comic book. Both before and after reading the books, the children were asked to complete a series of sentences, such as "I
want to _____ the book," choosing from pairs of possible
words, such as "read" or "tear." The tallies of aggressive responses indicated that children who read the war comic

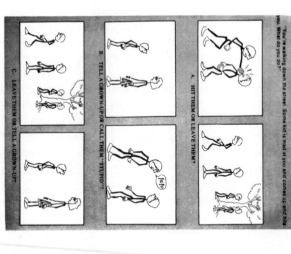

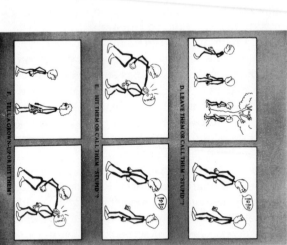

Source: A. D. Leifer & D. F. Roberts, *Children's Response to Television Violence*, 2 TELEVISION AND SOCIAL BEHAVIOR.

responded with aggressive words significantly more often than those who read *Gidget.* Note that, depending upon the year in which the experiment was conducted, there may also be substantial justification effects. The Green Berets were fighting the United States' battles in what was widely thought to be a moral war in the early and middle parts of the 1960s.

Print media experiments with adults offer similarly mixed results. These experiments often seem to test different conceptions of aggression from those tested in television studies, but they still lend tangential support to the violence hypothesis associated with the reading of violent material.

For example, Judith L. Fisher and Mary B. Harris ran a 2×2 design experiment, crossing insults or no insults to the subject with the reading of violent or nonviolent matter. Subjects were asked to select from a list of adjectives, including "stupid" and "valuable," to best describe the researcher and the project. Among insulted subjects, those who had read aggressive, violent matter selected more aggressive adjectives, but among noninsulted subjects, those who had read neutral matter selected more aggressive adjectives.[42] When the results of the two groups were combined, there was no significant difference between their responses. The experimenters provide only a few tentative and unsatisfactory explanations for the data.[43] The most plausible interpretation is that the data completely fail to support the violence hypothesis for reading in general. (Of course, one could use the data to conclude that for people who are most likely to be violent—those who have been provoked— the violence hypothesis garners some support.)

Michael Spiegler and Andrea Weiland[44] and Andrea Weiland's[45] experimental results are clearly consistent with the previously discussed Bandura, Ross, and Ross experiment on the punishing or rewarding of aggressive models.[46] Spiegler and Weiland's college-age subjects read a story about a series of conflicts and confrontations between a high-school principal and the student body president. The story had three variations: positive consequences, where the student body president was rewarded for confronting the principal; neutral consequences, where the student body president was neither rewarded nor punished; and negative consequences, where the student body president was punished for confronting the principal. Each subject read only one of the versions, and then answered a series of questions designed to elicit the likelihood that he or she would act as the student body president had. Those who read the story with positive consequences were more likely than the others to state that, in such circumstances, they too would confront and challenge the principal.

Although consistent with Bandura, Ross, and Ross, these results should be regarded with caution. Instead of physical or verbal violence, Spiegler and Weiland's work, as well as the very similar work of Weiland herself,[47] concentrated upon confrontation within an institutional (high school) setting. In addition, they measured self-reported willingness to act, rather than any actual activities.

Based on the foregoing material, one could conclude that viewing violent matter produces aggression but that reading violent matter (insofar as one "reads" a comic book) does not. However, a few factors suggest that this conclusion may not be warranted. First, there is only one laboratory experiment on reading that produces a clearly null result, and that result could be wrong. Though some research shows that a child's self-report on these questions correlates positively with knowledgeable adults' independent ratings of the child's aggressiveness,[48] data used by Tan and Scruggs to measure aggression may not be as accurate as direct observation. Second, there have been far fewer experiments concerning reading and aggression than concerning television and aggression. Third, and least important, Tan and Scruggs used a violent comic book that was sold well after the adoption of the comic book code,[49] and therefore the book was likely to contain relatively mild fare. Nevertheless, I will set aside these three objections, assume that the difference has been proven in the laboratory, and consider the normative significance of such a difference. But first I will consider the field work regarding television and print.

FIELD WORK

Field Experiments

Field experiments are conducted in "natural" settings such as homes or schools. This gives the researcher greater assurance that the results apply to the world at large. In a typical media field experiment the researcher controls the viewing diet of his subjects and observes their behavior, such as aggressive playtime activities. However, in natural settings, researchers have less control over crucial variables, providing some uncertainty regarding the accuracy of their results.

First, I will briefly review the results of field experiments concerning television (or film) and aggression. It appears that such field evidence may do little to support the television violence hypothesis. No such uncertainty exists about field experiments with print only because there are none. Consequently, I cannot compare broadcast and print. The television results will be reviewed only to illuminate an overall comparison—across laboratory experiments, field experiments, and field correlations—of the violence hypotheses for broadcast and print.

Perhaps the most famous field experiment, by Seymour Feshbach and Robert Singer,[50] was designed to test the catharsis theory—that watching violence reduces both the need to aggress and actual aggression. The experimenters controlled the television diets of several hundred boys living in one of three private schools or one of four boys' homes. Some boys were placed on an aggressive diet, including such programs as "Bonanza," "I Spy," and "The Rifleman." The remainder of the boys watched nonaggressive television, including "Andy Williams," "Gomer Pyle," and "Petticoat Junction." Houseparents, teachers, and proctors monitored and recorded "naturally" occurring violence involving the boys throughout the six-week experimental period. The results were ambiguous. Those in boys' homes who watched violent programs aggressed less than those who watched the nonaggressive diet, but the boys in private schools aggressed the same amount, regardless of what they saw. The results could be interpreted as some support for the null hypothesis, or the catharsis theory, or both.

Regardless of how they are interpreted, these results will probably bear little weight, for they have been strongly and effectively criticized. First, the boys watching the nonaggressive diet enjoyed their programs far less than the boys on the aggressive diet. They even protested the situation. This discontent might account for some of the aggression observed—a reaction against authority.[51] In addition, aggression toward their peers may have been a way of relieving high levels of boredom or frustration with the situation.[52] Second, when some of the boys assigned to the nonaggressive diet refused to cooperate unless they could watch "Batman," a very violent program, the researchers capitulated and placed Batman on the nonaggressive diet. Thus, the experiment was not a clear test of the effects of a nonaggressive diet.[53] Third, by yielding to the aggressive demands by the boys, the experimenters may have encouraged additional aggression in that group.[54] Fourth, the experiment may have been plagued by demand effects. The observers knew to which groups each subject belonged, and their ratings of the boys' aggressive acts may have been influenced by this knowledge. Furthermore, some of the boys guessed the purpose of the experiment, and those assigned the aggressive diet had incentives to demonstrate that the diet did not provoke aggression (so as to prevent the authorities from removing violent programs from their television diet after the termination of the experiment.)[55]

Other experimental field work has produced a very mixed picture. Three experiments, conducted without many of the flaws of Feshbach and Singer's work, seem to support the violence hypothesis.[56] Several other studies, however, plausibly support a null hypothesis.[57] Together, the field experiments present no clear conclusion.[58] One can state, with fair certainty, that the catharsis hypothesis garners little support. But field experiments offer little guidance in choosing between the null and violence hypotheses.

Field Correlations

In field correlations, the experimenter gathers data on a host of variables, including a child's television diet (often by asking the child or the parents what the child watches) and rates the child's aggressiveness (either by asking the child or his peers, teacher, or parents). In cross-sectional studies, researchers typically ask whether a child who watches more violent television also tends to be more aggressive, that is, whether the two variables correlate positively. A correlation coefficient always varies between one and negative one. If, for example, whenever a child has a 10 percent larger diet of violent programs he also is 10 percent more violent, the two variables are perfectly positively correlated, and their correlation coefficient is one. Conversely, if a 10 percent increase in watching violent programs is always associated with 10 percent less aggressive behavior, then the two variables are perfectly negatively correlated and have a correlation coefficient of negative one. Variables with more moderate relationships have correlation coefficients between the extremes. A coefficient of zero indicates that the variables have no correlation whatsoever. The null hypothesis in these studies almost always presumes no correlation.

A purely cross-sectional correlation approach does not actually demonstrate causation. If two variables, *a* and *b*, correlate positively, *a* might cause *b*, *b* might cause *a*, some third variable might cause both, or some combination of all three explanations might be correct. To complicate things further, the list of third variables is potentially infinite.

The only study that approaches a controlled test of the different effects of broadcast and print is an elaborate cross-sectional field correlation by William Belson,[59] financed entirely by the CBS television network. Belson gathered data on 1,600 London boys' behavior, beliefs, socioeconomic status, television, comic book, newspaper and motion picture diets, and other variables. He then estimated the probability that a large number of hypotheses, many of them versions of the violence hypothesis, were correct. Through an extremely complicated and technical process of controlling for the possible influence of third variables on both the violence hypothesis and the reverse of the violence hypothesis (that a taste for violent behavior leads to a taste for viewing or reading violence), Belson partly eliminated the causal inference problems normally associated with simple correlations.[60] This technique enabled Belson to generate probabilities for the truth of each hypothesis and, independently, its reverse. Thus, for each hypothesis and its reverse, there were four logical possibilities: (1) the data supported both the hypothesis and its reverse; (2) the data supported only the hypothesis; (3) the data supported only the reverse hypothesis; and (4) the data supported neither. Of course, the possibility that some unchecked third factor actually caused the observed phenomena could not be eliminated.

When Belson tested the violence hypothesis for television,[61] he found that the "evidence . . . is very strongly supportive of the hypothesis that high exposure to television violence increases the degree to which boys engage in serious violence. . . . [But] the reversed form of the hypothesis is *not* supported by the evidence."[62] "Serious violence" included frightening a boy by pretending to throw him over a balcony, stomping on a dog's tail, or firing a revolver at a person.[63] For less serious violence, the violence hypothesis garnered "moderate" support, but the reverse hypothesis could not be eliminated.[64]

Similar but not identical results emerged when Belson tested the violence hypothesis for comic books. He found that for the hypothesis that *"exposure to comics/comic books increases boys' violence at the serious level,* the evidence . . . gives a very large degree of support."[65] He suggested, however, some caution about this result, partly because the reverse hypothesis could not be discounted entirely. And, for less serious violence, Belson found that the data produced "a fairly large degree of support" for the violence hypothesis, but, again, the reverse could not be ruled out.

Belson also tested the violence hypothesis for newspapers. Here, too, the data gave "a fairly large degree of support" for the violence hypothesis for less serious forms of violence, although the reverse hypothesis could not be ruled out.[66] The data provided no support for the violence hypothesis for newspapers involving serious violence.

Last, Belson checked to see whether the results for any given medium could be merely a reflection of exposure to other media. He found that "exposure to television violence [was] very little correlated with exposure to other mass media,"[67] so the television results were reliable. Additionally, the print media results appeared untainted by subjects' television exposure.

Belson concluded that:

1 *At the level of boys' violence, considered generally.*
   . . . At this level, all four of the media hypotheses were supported by the evidence. For each of them there exists a possibility that to some small extent the support they receive is a reflection of the hypothesis working in reverse. But on balance, the tenability of each is advanced by the evidence. If anything, the support given to the TV violence hypothesis is a trifle less strong than that given to the hypotheses involving comics, violent films and newspapers respectively.

2 *At the level of "serious violence" by boys.* . . . With regard to serious violence by boys, the hypothesis featuring exposure to *television* violence got considerably more support from the evidence than did the hypothesis involving comics on the one hand or that involving violent films on the other. That involving newspapers can hardly be said to have been supported at all (i.e. at *this* level of violent behavior by boys).[68]

Unfortunately, Belson's work did not control for the quality of violence in the various media. For example, comic books were all considered violent, with no differentiation between types or amounts of violence. Belson's work also did not differentiate between violent and nonviolent newspaper stories. In contrast, Belson provided a very detailed taxonomy of television violence and constructed his tests around it. Because of this lack of uniformity, Belson's work was not a controlled test of the media. Nevertheless, because his work is the only one to use the same subject pool, sampling techniques, and data analysis to test the violence hypotheses for both television and print, its results are uniquely significant for my inquiry.

There have been many other field correlations of television and aggressive behavior.[69] On balance, they support the violence hypothesis moderately, although they conflict with one another to some degree.[70] Additionally, even where studies find positive correlations, their small correlation coefficients, between 0 and 0.2, indicate a weak relationship.[71] Because of these drawbacks, the other cross-sectional studies are only weak confirmation of the violence hypothesis.

Longitudinal surveys attempt to avoid some of the cross-sectional studies' problems in proving causation. A longitudinal survey gathers the same data as a cross-sectional work, but, unlike the cross-sectional work, the longitudinal survey gathers more than once, allowing long periods of time between data collections. Consider a hypothetical longitudinal survey that obtained data regarding the television diet, aggressive behavior, socioeconomic status, and other social variables of a set of children at two different times (t_1, t_2). If a violent television diet at t_1 correlates positively with aggressive behavior at t_2, but aggressive behavior at t_1 is uncorrelated with a violent television diet at t_2, then one might conclude that a violent television diet causes aggressive behavior but not vice versa. This is because antecedent variables (those at t_1) can cause subsequent variables (those at t_2), but not the other way around. Of course, not all doubt can be eliminated with this method, for some third variable might cause both a violent television diet and later aggressive behavior.

The first longitudinal study[72] of television violence produced results exactly like those described above. The researchers first studied a group of third graders and then studied the same group ten years later in the "thirteenth" grade. They concluded that the data supported the violence hypothesis. Unfortunately, this study also suffers from moderately serious defects. When studying the third graders (t_1), the researchers assessed television diets by asking each subject's mother to list the subject's three favorite shows. However, ten years later (t_2), the researchers asked *each subject* to name his *four* favorite shows. The study's results could be due, in part, to increased sensitivity in the assessment of television diets at t_2. In addition, the aggression measure changed slightly. The third-grade aggression ratings were derived from reports of peers in the same class, while ten years later "the number of possible peers any subject could nominate was expanded beyond his own third-grade classmates to include his classmates through high school."[73] These two defects in the study partially detract from the force of its support for the violence hypothesis.

There have been other large longitudinal studies. Of these, several support the violence hypothesis,[74] at least one solidly supports the null hypothesis,[75] and one gives some support to both the violence and null hypotheses.[76] Together, these studies present a very mixed picture, with the balance probably marginally in favor of the violence hypothesis.

In sum, field experiments do not help one select between the violence and null hypotheses for television, while both cross-sectional and longitudinal field correlations provide the violence hypothesis for television with nominal support.

How do these results compare with those of field work done on print media? There are only three field studies on print and aggression (other than Belson's) and all are cross-sectional studies of comic books. One found a correlation between reading "harmful" comic books and juvenile delinquency.[77] The other two studies controlled for various social variables; one found no significant association between exposure to crime comics and self-reported delinquency,[78] while the other found a positive relationship for girls, but not for boys. Even if a correlation had been found in both studies, one would still not know whether the violence hypothesis or its reverse was being tested. Thus, these studies provide little guidance for choosing between the null and the violence hypotheses.

I will completely discount the clinical data approach, as embodied in the famous work of New York psychiatrist Frederic Wertham.[79] Wertham "proved" that reading comic books tended to cause delinquency by assembling some clinical cases in which he was certain that there was a connection between the two. Regardless of whether or not he was correct that comic book reading leads to bad effects (and this is by no means an easy issue), and regardless of how politically appealing his message was,[80] his methodology provides no convincing evidence of the general tendency of comic books to cause delinquency or aggression in the population at large. To formulate social policy from one's conclusions, one must instead sample from large populations and subject the data to appropriate statistical analysis.[81] The defects in Wertham's methodology have been previously noted in the social psychological literature.[82]

There is another type of correlational study—sometimes called "quasi-experimental"—that provides no help. These works use aggregate data to analyze whether people imitate widely publicized acts of violence. For example, such studies try to determine whether widely publicized boxing matches cause a rise in the murder rate or suicide rate by comparing murder and suicide statistics for the ten days following widely publicized boxing matches with the "normal" murder and suicide rates. In the words of James N. Baron and Peter C. Reiss in the most recent review of the subject, *Same Time, Next Year: Aggregate Analyses of the Mass Media and Violent Behavior:*[83]

> Aggregate studies of imitative violence typically use two research strategies to measure imitative responses to media violence. The first compares mortality in a prior control period to mortality immediately following a highly publicized violent media event (the experimental period). The second methodology uses interrupted time-series regression techniques to correlate levels of violent activity, net of other predictable effects, with dummy variables that purportedly represent period-by-period responses to the violent event. In both approaches, mortality

trends after a media stimulus are compared to pre-
dictions from a baseline model or control period. De-
viations from the control are taken to represent
"treatment effects" aggregated across individuals.

Such studies cannot help to justify differential control of the
content of the media because the widely reported violent acts
are reported in both broadcast and print media.[84]

EVALUATING THE EVIDENCE

Is the violence hypothesis for television (VH-TV) more tenable
than the violence hypothesis for print (VH-P)? Laboratory evidence supports the VH-TV substantially more than the VH-P.
But field experiments provide no basis for choosing between
the VH-TV and the null (that is, no correlation) hypothesis,
and there are no field experiments on print. In field correlations, Belson's work, which clearly provides the most useful
data, finds the VH-TV slightly less probable than the VH-P for
less serious forms of violence, but more probable than the VH-
P for serious violence. Other cross-sectional field work provides only weak support for the VH-TV over the null hypothesis
for television, and virtually no support for the VH-P over the
null hypothesis. Lastly, longitudinal field correlations offer
only moderate support for the VH-TV. There are no longitudinal field works for print.

At this point, the burden of proof becomes crucial. Where
should we place the burden? There are at least two different
ways to assign it. Cost considerations suggest we place the
burden on those who would further differential treatment. Alternatively, we could place the burden of proof on those who
would disturb the presumptions supporting the status quo.
Just as in the evaluation of sexually explicit material, I will
choose no particular burden of proof; instead I will show
which burdens the evidence overcomes and which it does not.

Placing the burden on those who would demonstrate differential effects for the media makes the issue very close. On
balance, the evidence probably fails to prove differential effects because only laboratory evidence suggests that the

VH-TV is substantially more plausible than the VH-P, and Belson's work, in general, reveals no overall difference in support for the two hypotheses. One could also, quite rationally, hold the opposite view, however, and find that such evidence does show differential effects.

Alternatively, if the presumption is that the VH-TV is more likely than the VH-P, and that the burden is on those who would show equality, then the burden is not sustained. One would conclude that the VH-TV is more likely than the VH-P. Only if the presumption were that the VH-P is more likely than the VH-TV—and no one seems to believe this—would the burden be sustained and equality demonstrated.

IMPLICATIONS

If we assume the evidence shows the VH-TV to be more plausible than the VH-P, what forms of differential regulation are justified? VH-TV studies actually offer very little for purposes of policymaking.[85] The studies all measured subjects' aggressive or violent behavior. But the studies must give information about behavior that is normatively bad, before they can provide any policy guidance. Can violence be good, or at least not bad? Violence in justifiable self-defense or in defense of a third party arguably garners little social disapproval. Chopping wood with an axe, knocking down a dilapidated building, blasting a quarry, and tackling a halfback also seem innocuous to most people. To rule out these and similar examples of unobjectionable aggression, one must proffer a reasonably precise definition of bad violence. Krattenmaker and Powe, after a lengthy investigation, proposed the following definition: "the purposeful, illegal infliction of pain for personal gain or gratification that is intended to harm the victim and is accomplished in spite of societal sanctions against it."[86] Their definition describes a large class of normatively unappealing behavior.[87] Unfortunately, none of the studies reviewed above focused solely on such behavior.

The laboratory studies, which produced the strongest evidence in favor of the VH-TV, studied normatively innocuous examples of violence and aggression. For example, Bandura, Ross, and Ross[88] observed such activities as children hitting a Bobo doll, sitting on Bobo and calling it "stupid clown," and taking imaginary shots with a dart gun. None of these acts were against the laboratory rules, and none of them hurt anyone or even anything. When a live clown replaced the Bobo doll, the results gained a bit of significance because a human was taking blows. However, hitting the live clown was not against laboratory rules, and may have been implicitly sanctioned by the experimental treatment. (Indeed, why else would the human dress as a Bobo?) Using a Buss aggression machine helps only slightly, for even though subjects may believe they are actually hurting someone, they still know that they are acting within the rules of the experiment. Indeed, in some of the experiments, subjects may even administer shocks so as to aid the experimenter's learning and thus benefit society.[89]

The field studies focused more directly on bad aggression, but they gave no real support to the VH-TV over the null hypothesis, and thus are of no use here. The field correlations provided moderate support for the VH-TV, but they typically included such items as forceful self-defense,[90] or verbal aggression, such as "saying mean things,"[91] within their overall aggression measures. Including such items dilutes the normative significance of the results.

Of course, one can hardly expect social scientists to routinely observe bad aggressive behavior. Instead, one must inquire whether the results, either for innocuous laboratory aggression or for self-reports of both bad and innocuous aggression in the field, apply directly to performing bad aggressive acts (application hypothesis). In other words, are the social scientists measuring things so fundamentally different from the target of concern that their studies provide no guidance? For the laboratory studies a special concern is the possibility of experimental effects. One cannot be certain that the behavioral tendencies observed in the laboratory will also manifest themselves in natural settings. Several considerations counsel caution: subjects watch the screen more in the laboratory than in natural settings; experimental films are quite short, and are shown without commercials; subjects are usually given an immediate opportunity to aggress in the laboratory; and, as previously discussed, subjects are not punished for acts of aggression in the laboratory, while they often are in natural surroundings.

There is no widely accepted theory to resolve these issues. Thus one must proceed on a combination of intuition and guesswork. My guess is that the application hypothesis is only true to a very slight degree, and that the research reviewed above is therefore correspondingly less important for policymaking. Nevertheless, even if one concludes that the application hypothesis is true, there are other reasons to be very cautious about using the studies of the VH-TV for policy guidance.

First, regardless of the relative appeal of the VH-TV over the VH-P, the VH-TV's absolute appeal is only moderate. The studies present a mixed picture, and those field studies that validate the VH-TV nevertheless report small correlation coefficients.

Second, virtually all of the evidence presented is published in professional journals and is thus subject to journal demand effects. It is much easier to publish studies that find a statistically significant difference from the treatment variables than to publish articles that confirm the null hypothesis.[92] Because academic departments reward members who publish articles, the prejudice against the null hypothesis may skew scientists' decisions to complete partially run experiments, or even to record the results of studies that support the null hypothesis. Last, experimenter demand effects might also have altered the pattern of results. Psychology experiments often produce results that conform to the desires of those running the experiment, and most of the psychologists working in this field propose theories validating the violence hypothesis.[93] All of these concerns suggest that we should be quite cautious about using the social science literature for policy guidance.

If, nonetheless, we still want to rely upon the VH-TV studies for policy guidance, what policies should we adopt? The obvious possibilities, all of which have been discussed at a general level, include banning or zoning violent programming, increasing parental control over children's television diets, and requiring balanced programming.

All of these possibilities have problems. Banning violence, perhaps an overly harsh reaction to studies with such low correlation coefficients, has both definitional and slippery slope problems. Defining prohibited programming without inadvertently including socially unobjectionable material could be very difficult. The research is of little help, as few studies have focused on the precise nature of the violent programming that can trigger the VH-TV.[94] The closely related problems of defining obscene material are legendary. Justice Potter Stewart, for example, in his concurring opinion in *Jacobellis v. Ohio*,[95] noted that the Court, in attempting to define obscenity, "was faced with the task of trying to define what may be indefinable." He concluded: "I shall not today attempt further to define the kinds of material I understand to be embraced within that shorthand description; and perhaps I could never succeed in intelligibly doing so. But I know it when I see it, and the motion picture involved in this case is not that."

Further, absolute bans on violence might completely prevent the presentation of otherwise worthwhile stories or themes. Finally, it would be necessary to guard against a slide down the slippery slope to prohibition of content that produces results not nearly so universally disapproved.

If the definitional and slippery slope problems are overcome (or ignored), yet a total ban appears too harsh, then limiting violent material to certain hours might seem an attractive alternative. If the purpose of such regulation were to preclude children from viewing violent material, it would be necessary to zone violence into very late hours.[96] Alternatively, if the purpose were to help parents control their children's diet, it would be necessary only to restrict such programming to those hours when parents tend to be home.

Parental control also could be increased by redesigning broadcasting institutions. This would include not only zoning violent matter, but also redesigning receivers and video cassette recorders to allow greater parental control.[97] Such changes would be costly and therefore would need to produce large benefits to be justified. If most parents preferred to restrict their children's diet of violence, these changes might work. However, such reforms would be useless if the attempted restriction provoked enough familial disharmony to dissuade most parents from enforcing the restrictive television diet.

Warnings in program guides prior to or during violent programs promise little help. Children would probably regard such warnings as advertisements. In addition, such information would be of only marginal use to adults without effective control over their children's access to television.

Another possibility is balanced programming, which includes a couple of different options. One option is to force broadcasters to program antiviolent, prosocial material.[98] However, no studies demonstrate that this would effectively counter the influence of violence. Further, there is already a tremendous amount of nonviolent, prosocial programming on the air. Until someone can explain, with evidentiary support, just how much prosocial programming is needed to offset violent programming, this option probably reduces to doing nothing.

Balancing might also include some other sort of affirmative intervention, such as educating children to understand the lack of reality in television programs. Recent work along this line is very promising. L. Rowell Huesmann and associates have reported the results of an attitude modification field experiment upon first and third graders that was very successful at eliminating the effects of televised violence on the subjects.[99] An inexpensive educational scheme, based on Huesmann's attitude modification experiment, might provide a very attractive policy structure.

In sum, there is little reason to rely on the surveyed empirical work to make policy. Such work has very limited application to normative questions, and reveals only slight modification of human behavior. If, however, such studies are used to frame policy, they suggest the zoning of violence, in combination with prosocial intervention, such as teaching children to interpret television violence.

Seven Dirty Words:

7 Accessibility

A number of rationales for treating the media differently are products of perceived differences in the accessibility of print and broadcast. Some of these accessibility rationales focus on the ability of the communication, particularly of sexually explicit or violent material, to produce bad behavior. The rate at which a communication inspires antisocial acts by its audience is a function of both the content and the accessibility of the message. For example, if a message is never received, it cannot affect anyone's behavior. Other accessibility rationales appeal to norms of liberty and privacy, sometimes relying upon the freedom of parents to control their children's exposure to sensitive matters.

ADULTS

The first rationale for distinguishing print from broadcast stems from Justice Stevens' opinion in *FCC v. Pacifica Foundation,*[1] the "seven dirty words" case. A New York radio station affiliated with the Pacifica network had aired George Carlin's "Filthy Word" monologue about "the words you couldn't say on the public, ah, airwaves," in which Carlin repeated the words (fuck, shit, etc.) many times. The FCC ruled that Pacifica could be punished for airing the monologue. On appeal the Supreme Court held that it was constitutional to punish a radio station for airing this "indecent" matter, although a printed version of the monologue could not be suppressed constitutionally. Justice Stevens tried to explain the distinction:

> The reasons for these distinctions are complex, but two have relevance to the present case. First, the broadcast media have established a uniquely pervasive presence in the lives of all Americans. Patently offensive, indecent material presented over the

119

airwaves confronts the citizen, not only in public, but
also in the privacy of the home, where the individual's
right to be left alone plainly outweighs the First
Amendment rights of an intruder.[2]

This "pervasiveness" rationale, anchored in privacy, suggests
that only broadcast materials are "uniquely" accessible, particularly in the home. To gain access to television or radio, all
one has to do is reach out and flick a switch, but to gain access
to print, one has to walk down to the corner bookstore.

This argument seems to rely on the comparison of different scenarios; if we compare similar scenarios the differences
between print and broadcast disappear. First, printed publications can be delivered to the home and pushed inside through
the mail slot. Indeed, a huge volume of newspapers and magazines, much of it including sexual or violent content, is distributed in exactly this fashion. Second, radio and television
communications cannot be received in the home unless one
has already brought a radio or television into the home and
turned it on; similarly, printed publications will not ordinarily
be delivered unless they first have been ordered.[3]

The symmetry between print and broadcast makes it un-
necessary to decide, for the purposes of this book, whether
Justice William Brennan's argument in the *Pacifica* dissent
that the decision to turn on the radio equals a "decision to take
part, if only as a listener, in an ongoing public discourse"[4] is
correct or not. If Justice Brennan is correct, as he almost certainly is, then one could say the same thing about subscribing
to *Penthouse* magazine by mail. Similarly, if he is wrong, and
the government may properly invoke listeners' privacy interests when they listen to the radio, then the government may
invoke these same privacy interests to control the content of
printed publications. Therefore, this accessibility argument
has no significance for distinguishing print and broadcast.

A second accessibility argument, termed "captive audience," focuses on the relative inability of viewers to refuse to
receive broadcast messages. Television viewers and radio listeners receive messages, often commercials, before they can
change the channel. To protect their autonomy, the argument

runs, we should control broadcast content. Such an argument applies equally to print. People see advertisements in newspapers and magazines before they can avert their eyes. Therefore, no special regulation of broadcast can be justified.

A more extreme version of this argument suggests that television, unlike print, is hypnotic and addictive and thus viewers cannot abstain from watching.* But insofar as this argument is based on low-involvement learning or dot-scan image processing, it was previously discussed and rejected in chapter 4. Insofar as the argument reduces to a naked assertion that video is addictive, the crucial question is whether print and broadcast are differently addictive. I have found no data on this point; and until someone produces some, I will put aside this argument.

A closely related argument for differential content control would claim that television violence and pornography are more addictive than their printed counterparts. Assuming that printed and televised violence and pornography are equally effective at inspiring bad behavior in a given addict (see chapters 5 and 6), television would produce a higher ultimate rate of bad behavior. If the argument's basic factual assertion—that televised violence and pornography are more addictive—is correct, then this might provide a justification for regulating broadcast more strictly.

Because I have found no comparative data on this point, I will make some reasonable assumptions about the comparative qualities of addiction to print and video violence and pornography. First, more people become addicted to watching violence or pornography on television than become addicted to

---

*We can object to the addictive aspects of the media on grounds of autonomy, irrespective of any other behavioral effects. If we conceive of autonomy as including the ability to form and act on preferences for future preferences, then the addict has given up some future autonomy because he or she will be incapable of acting on future preferences for nonaddiction. If, however, we restrain the addict from becoming addicted, we limit a potential addict's present autonomy. If we believe the loss in present autonomy may be justified by preserving the addict's future autonomy (because autonomy is thereby increased), then we may justifiably withhold the source of the addiction.

reading it. Second, because there are few people in either category, the difference in size of the two groups is very small. Third, the sociopathic characteristics of the two groups are identical. Under these assumptions it would be difficult to find measures that address the basic problem of addiction among a small percentage of the population but that are different for the two media. The most obvious responses—attempting to screen the population for addicts, or controlling content—apply equally to both media. Therefore, this argument does not justify differential content control.

A slightly different version of the captive audience argument concentrates on the listener's inability to weed out unwanted "indecent" material from his or her viewing diet. Again, Justice Stevens:

> Because the broadcast audience is constantly tuning in and out, prior warnings cannot completely protect the listener or viewer from unexpected program content. To say that one may avoid further offense by turning off the radio when he hears indecent language is like saying that the remedy for an assault is to run away after the first blow.[5]

Justice Stevens's argument appeals more to notions of personal dignity and freedom than to concerns about any behavioral effects produced by the unwanted material. Because there are no serious behavioral issues stemming from brief, unwanted exposures, the following discussion addresses only personal dignity and freedom.

As with the addiction argument, one must question whether Justice Stevens has distinguished broadcast from print. Do readers ever encounter unwanted, indecent printed material? Certainly they do outside their homes. One can hardly walk through the streets of major American cities without seeing pictures of naked men and women, often in sexual poses, on the covers of newspapers and magazines that are sold in vending machines. Within the home, people may get unwanted publications through the mail. Offended recipients can ask the post office to order the sender to refrain from mailing anything to them in the future or be subject to sanctions.[6] In addition, federal statutes allow one who does not wish to receive any "sexually oriented advertisements" to place his name on a list that is kept by the post office. Any person who mails a sexually oriented advertisement to a person whose name has been on the list for at least thirty days may be subject to sanctions.[7] Finally, federal statutes absolutely prohibit the mailing of any obscene matter.[8]

In most respects, these conditions also apply to broadcast. In public, people are constantly exposed to various unwanted broadcast messages. In the home, one might inadvertently come across some unwanted material while changing channels, but one could avoid such unwanted material in the future by checking program listings or by not turning the set on until the desired channel was selected. Of course, one wishing to scan all channels with a receiver and then select the one that is pleasing would run a high risk of hearing unwanted matter. People listening to car radios might behave this way. But this procedure roughly corresponds to ordering magazines at random to scan the available printed publications—one would run a high risk of getting something unwanted. Of course, if there were no statutory prohibition, one's favorite station could suddenly start broadcasting indecent matter, just as the *Wall Street Journal* could unexpectedly publish it.

In this area, the primary difference between print and broadcast seems to be the relative cost of scanning broadcast stations to determine content versus that of ordering magazines at random to find out what they contain. Scanning broadcast is much cheaper, so one might expect listeners or viewers to encounter much more unwanted material (in the home) than would readers. This difference could justify a broadcast requirement that all stations that broadcast sexually explicit matter (or other material deemed objectionable) locate in a small, well-defined section of the spectrum, so that scanners could avoid such matter. If all radio stations carrying sexually explicit matter were located between 535 KHz and 600 KHz, someone scanning the dial could avoid this section of the radio spectrum. This would parallel segregating "adult" (sexually oriented) books into separate bookstores, or separate sections of bookstores.

CHILDREN

Perhaps one must regulate broadcast more strictly than print because:

> broadcasting is uniquely accessible to children, even those too young to read. Although Cohen's written message ["Fuck the Draft"] might have been incomprehensible to a first grader, Pacifica's broadcast could have enlarged a child's vocabulary in an instant. Other forms of offensive expression may be withheld from the young without restricting the expression at its source. Bookstores and motion picture theaters, for example, may be prohibited from making indecent material available to children. We held in *Ginsberg v. New York*, 390 U.S. 629, that the government's interest in the "well-being of its youth" and in supporting "parents' claim to authority in their own household" justified the regulation of otherwise protected expression. Id., at 640 and 639. . . . The ease with which children may obtain access to broadcast material, coupled with the concerns recognized in *Ginsberg*, amply justify special treatment of indecent broadcasting.[9]

The quoted language implicitly refers to at least two different arguments. First, assuming that exposure to profanity, pornography, and violence is bad for children, broadcasting such material is more pernicious than printing it because broadcast is more accessible to children than print. Second, the state has a quasi-parental interest in ensuring that children are reared correctly. Because broadcast is uniquely accessible to children it can interfere with their proper upbringing. To protect them, the state may regulate broadcast content more strictly than print.

As will become clear below, I believe that the first argument, given its assumption that profanity, pornography, and violence are harmful, might justify some safeguards on the broadcast of violence, but the second argument justifies no differential treatment of print and broadcast.

Television may be more accessible to children than print either because broadcast is easier to understand or because it is easier to obtain. Is broadcast really easier to understand? Probably it is, because many children are illiterate. (Indeed, all start that way.) For this "problem," pictorial magazines provide an accessible alternative source for erotica, but not necessarily for violent matter. There are virtually no violent "picture books" that are analogous to erotic books and magazines. To be appreciated, violent printed matter seems to require a much greater ability to read. This situation might be the product of current institutions. Prior to the adoption of the comic book code,[10] there was a great deal of explicit violence in printed publications. Yet marginal reading ability was required to appreciate these, too, and today there are no magazines that picture violence as graphically as some do sexual material.

Is broadcast easier for children to obtain than print? Currently the answer for violence is "yes," but for profanity and pornography the opposite is true. However, altering institutional safeguards could change these results. For example, if the federal statutes outlawing broadcast pornography[11] were to be repealed and such material were to be freely broadcast, it would be more accessible to children than printed pornography because there are institutional safeguards against children obtaining sexually explicit printed matter. Children who obtain sexually explicit books and magazines must usually do so with the aid, or at least negligence, of an adult. There are similar safeguards against children obtaining pornography on videocassette. A substantial volume of "hard-core" (explicit and unmistakable presentation of actual intercourse) is sold in stores to adults, only. None of these materials are supposed to be sold directly to children. Therefore, an adult—either a salesperson or the child's parent or guardian—usually must, perhaps unwittingly, help the child obtain the material.

In contrast, broadcast pornography would be very easily available to children. No formal institution would stand in children's way. Indeed, moderately explicit violent matter, easily understandable by illiterate children, is already televised every day. This hypothetical situation shows that, as institutions change, the relative availability of print and broadcast changes.

To show that broadcast need not be easier to obtain than print, I will discuss hypothetical rules for broadcast, closely modeled on the rules for print. Under these rules, broadcast stations that transmit objectionable matter could be allowed to broadcast anything that would be legal if printed, but such stations would be concentrated in one section of the spectrum. Receivers capable of decoding this portion of this spectrum would not be sold to customers under eighteen years of age. These rules, together with the use of television locks—devices that temporarily disable a television set—would provide a roughly equal treatment of the two media. Of course, even if one were to institute such precautions, children would continue to obtain some video pornography and violence, just as they now obtain some printed pornography. But with this relatively equal institutional treatment, children would be equally able to obtain broadcast and print pornography, profanity and violence. In addition, as I will show below, the controls would be more effective for violence than for pornography.

First, consider pornography. Children interested in sex are often at least ten years of age. These children will tend to be clever enough to conspire with or trick adults into obtaining erotica for them. But there is no reason to suspect that such children will be much more adept at obtaining one medium rather than the other. Older children will likely manage to view and hear substantial amounts of broadcast erotica and read similar amounts of printed matter. In sum, under such hypothetical controls, children would likely have equal and substantial access to both print and broadcast erotica.

In contrast, children's interest in violent material probably begins at a much earlier age than does their intense, active interest in erotica. But young children are likely to be much less adept at circumventing institutional controls. Young children, unlike older ones, are unlikely to obtain receivers that can pick up broadcasts of restricted material, making the restrictions on violence very effective, unless parents help make the violence available. Under the hypothetical rules, however, it would be fairly easy to restrict a child's diet, and probably most parents would do so. Because young children are more likely to be illiterate, thereby restricting the usefulness of written substitutes, they would likely have equally poor access to print. Further, as previously noted, there are fewer printed pictures of violence that illiterate children can obtain. Of course, older children interested in violence could circumvent restrictive institutions to obtain this material as well as erotica.

Would profanity be equally available to children in print and broadcast? Yes, because young children would likely be unable to circumvent safeguards, and probably would have little interest in doing so. Older children might have a moderate interest in profanity, but would be equally adept at obtaining it in print and broadcast.

In sum, these hypothetical rules for broadcast, modeled on the rules for print, would likely equalize the availability of profanity, pornography and violence in broadcast and print. Therefore, the argument that broadcast of these materials may be prohibited because of their unique availability does not necessarily work.

The other argument—that broadcast is much easier to understand—is true for violent programming. Broadcast violence is much easier than print for young children to understand. However, with a change in institutions like those described by the hypothetical rules, violent matter would be very difficult for young children to obtain, so its understandability would not necessarily justify additional restrictions on broadcast. Only with an extremely permissive set of institutions, such as the present set that makes broadcast violence easy for young children to obtain, would broadcast's understandability justify extra safeguards.

Justice Stevens next defended regulating only broadcasting by invoking the state's quasi-parental responsibility. The

state has an interest in ensuring that children are raised properly. Because broadcast is uniquely pernicious, the argument
runs, the state should control broadcast more strictly than
print.

Such an argument might be explained in terms of economic efficiency, or the rights of parents, or the elimination of
bad behavior. An examination of each of these, however, will
demonstrate that this argument fails to justify different treatment of the two media. A simple efficiency argument would
assume that all parents wish to prohibit their children from
obtaining pornography, violence, or profanity, and that no
adults wish to obtain such material. Assuming that children's
preferences for such matter count for nothing, it would be quite
efficient for the state to prohibit the broadcast of pornography,
violence, and profanity, thereby saving parents the trouble and
expense of locking the set. If, alternatively, some adults do
wish to see such material, the interests of the adults could be
outweighed by the interests of the parents who desire a ban,
thereby producing the efficient prohibition.

The extent to which such an efficiency argument would
apply to print would depend on whether parents have similar
preferences for controlling their children's access to print and
broadcast, and whether adults have similar demand for print
and broadcast violence, pornography, and profanity. There is
no data on either of these matters, but we can make some reasonable assumptions. Although parents have widely varying
desires for restricting older children's access to violence, pornography, and profanity, the vast majority wish to prevent
young children from obtaining this stuff. Because broadcast is
much easier for young children to understand than print, most
parents have stronger preferences for withholding broadcast
than print. If these two assumptions are correct, banning violence, pornography, and profanity in broadcasts would produce greater benefits than would a similar ban in print.

Such a ban, however, would also produce greater costs in
broadcast than in print. Undoubtedly many adults wish to obtain such matter and, as I concluded earlier in this chapter, the
twenty million functionally illiterate adults probably prefer

broadcast to print. Banning broadcast would probably reduce utility more than would banning print.

In sum, restricting the content of broadcast would likely produce greater benefits and greater costs than would restricting print. An efficiency rationale, which requires that benefits be greater than costs, gains strength as benefits increasingly outdistance costs. The efficiency argument for restricting broadcast would be stronger if and only if, in moving from a ban on print to a ban on broadcast, benefits were to increase more than costs. My analysis, however, does not illuminate this crucial point. I cannot show, without specific data, whether benefits increase more than costs or vice versa. Therefore, until someone proffers such data, the efficiency version of Justice Stevens's argument will fail to justify differential content control.

A similar argument, based on the rights of parents to raise their children in any manner they wish, free from interference by broadcasters or print publishers, applies to both broadcast and print and provides no justification for differential content control. If parents have the right to control absolutely what their children may see on the television or hear on the radio, and the state must preclude the broadcast of offensive matter so as to enforce parents' rights, then strict control of broadcast could be justified. In a parallel fashion, if parents have the right to control absolutely what their children may read, and the state need preclude the publication of offensive matter so as to enforce parents' rights, then strict control of print may be justified. If one were to believe that parents have the right to control children's viewing fare, but not reading fare (or vice versa), these rights arguments would justify different treatment of the two media. However, until someone provides a convincing justification for such a strangely bifurcated set of parental rights, Justice Stevens's argument will apply equally to print and broadcast.

Finally, the state might prohibit the broadcast or publication of violence, pornography, or profanity, despite parents' wishes to expose their children to such material, because it harms the children. The state often terminates a natural parent's right to control the child if it is in the child's "best interests." There is no reason that the state could not try to reverse, at a more general level, parental judgments that are bad for children. Such a sentiment pervades the majority opinion in *Pacifica*. Justice Brennan believed that the majority failed to appreciate the desire of some parents to expose their children to the profanity in the Carlin monologue. However, the majority opinion, which did not explicitly acknowledge this argument, can be read to approve the FCC's overriding of such parental judgments, so as to avoid, for example, enlarging "a child's vocabulary in an instant."[12] Such an argument could support differential content only if parents had a greater propensity to give children harmful broadcast than print; or if one medium were more harmful because it was more easily understood; or if one medium were more harmful because it more effectively manipulated children's minds. The second and third reasons have already been discussed. The first seems somewhat unlikely. To the extent that it is true, it probably stems from a slightly higher marginal cost associated with showing a late night broadcast to a child than with showing him or her an offensive printed publication. If the child is not awake, one must tape the late night broadcast, but the adult need merely show the magazine or book to the child after the parent has already purchased the material. Of course, if the child is awake late at night, or if the parent would not have purchased the printed matter but for the wish to expose the child to it, print and broadcast would have similar marginal costs. In all, these differences seem so small that they cannot justify different treatment of broadcast and print.

Accessibility arguments for erotica, based either on plausible, general norms of preventing bad behavior or on liberty and privacy, produce no justification for differential treatment of the media. Accessibility arguments for violence, however, might suggest stricter regulation of broadcast than of print.

Conclusion

I have surveyed the most commonly suggested rationales for controlling the content of broadcast differently from the content of print. Although none of the scarcity rationales, spectrum management rationales, or the rationale about television's unfair persuasive power support treating print and broadcast differently, certain arguments dealing with the effects of, or access to, violent matter suggest minor differences in treatment. Still none of the rationales surveyed even approaches justifying the status quo. In particular, one might wish to zone violent matter into the late hours of the evening. Additionally, one might confine such matter to certain frequencies (channels) and allow only adults to purchase receivers that can decode these signals. But my analysis provides no substantial support for any other sharp difference in controlling the content of broadcast and print. In particular, rationales built on economic efficiency, sex, violence, and accessibility to children all fail to support the existence of an FCC that licenses broadcasters and evaluates their broadcast content under a "public interest" standard.

I have surveyed the most commonly mentioned (and most persuasive) rationales—economic efficiency, pernicious effects of erotica and violent material, and accessibility to children—and have found them all wanting. A full examination of the rationales for treating the content of print and broadcast differently might conceivably include a study of the differential effects, if any, of print and broadcast on political behavior, sex, and age role stereotyping, children's learning abilities,[1] consumption patterns, and so forth. If someone claims that one or another of these unexplored rationales can justify additional content control, he or she must now come forward and offer his or her proof. Until that time, however, anyone who cherishes the free market in print must regard the regulation of broadcasting as unjustified.

131

Notes

INTRODUCTION

1. Communications Act of 1934, 47 U.S.C.A. § 301 (West Supp. 1984) (FCC Act), requires the licensing of radio stations. The traditional understanding of the first amendment regards prior restraint or licensing of printed publications as forbidden. *See* Near v. Minnesota, 283 U.S. 697 (1931); New York Times Co. v. United States, 403 U.S. 713 (1971); Minneapolis Star and Tribune Co. v. Minnesota Comm'r of Revenue, 103 S.Ct. 1365 (1983).

2. Red Lion Broadcasting Co. v. FCC, 395 U.S. 367 (1969).

3. 47 U.S.C.A. § 309(a) (West Supp. 1984).

4. The Supreme Court has ruled that right-of-reply statutes are unconstitutional as applied to newspapers but that the same rules applied to broadcasters are perfectly acceptable. *Compare* Red Lion, 395 U.S. 367 *with* Miami Herald Publishing Co. v. Tornillo, 418 U.S. 241 (1974).

5. More complete historical treatments of this subject may be found in Coase, *The Federal Communications Commission,* 2 J.L. & Econ. 1, 1–7 (1959) and G. Archer, History of Radio to 1926 (1938).

6. Pub. L. No. 69–632, 44 Stat. 1162 (1927).

7. An alternative, which is mentioned only to highlight the contrast, would have the government creating a Federal Paper Commission (FPC) to regulate paper in a manner analogous to the regulation of spectrum. The FPC example may be found in B. Owen, Economics and Freedom of Expression 90 (1975).

8. Lee Bollinger's important article, *Freedom of the Press and Public Access: Toward a Theory of Partial Regulation of the Mass Media,* 75 Mich. L. Rev. 1 (1976), concludes that, although there are no relevant differences between printed publications and broadcasting, it is both constitutional and (probably) advisable to treat the media differently. I discuss his argument in chapter 4.

9. *See supra* note 2 and accompanying text.

10. 395 U.S. 367 (1969).

11. 47 U.S.C.A. § 301 (West Supp. 1984).

12. On this theory, *see generally,* United Church of Christ v. FCC, 359 F.2d 994, 1003 (D.C. Cir. 1966); Robinson, *The FCC and the First Amendment: Observations on 40 Years of Radio and Television Regulation,* 52 Minn. L. Rev. 67, 151–54 (1967); Sullivan, *Editorials and Controversies: The Broadcasting Dilemma,* 32 Geo. Wash. L. Rev. 719, 761–66 (1964); Van Alstyne, *The Mobeius Strip of the First Amendment: Perspectives on Red Lion,* 29 S.C. L. Rev. 539, 565 (1978). *See also* Reich, *The New Property,* 73 Yale L.J. 733 (1964).

CHAPTER 1

1. Some of my discussion of the scarcity rationale has been adapted from that found in Coase, *The Federal Communications Commission,* 2 J.L. & Econ. 1, 12–40 (1959), and Polsby, *Candidate Access to the Air: The Uncertain Future of Broadcaster Discretion,* 1981 Sup. Ct. Rev. 223.

2. 319 U.S. 190 (1943).

3. *Id.* at 226 (turning away a first amendment claim) (emphasis added).

4. *Id.* at 228 (Murphy, J. dissenting).

5. 395 U.S. 367 (1969).

6. *See* FCC v. Pacifica Found., 438 U.S. 726 (1978).

7. *See* Consolidated Edison Co. v. Pub. Serv. Comm'r, 447 U.S. 530 (1980); *see also* R. Liebert, J. Sprafkin & E. Davidson, The Early Window 11 (2d ed. 1978) (citing scarcity as the rationale for regulating broadcasting, and not print).

8. 104 S.Ct. 3106 (1984).

9. *Id.* at 3116 n.11.

10. Coase, *supra* note 1, at 12–13.

11. Coase, *supra* note 1, at 25–35.

12. *Freedom of Expression: Hearings before the Senate Comm. on Commerce, Science, and Transportation* 97th Cong., 2d Sess. 110 (1982) (testimony of William Van Alstyne) [hereinafter cited as *Hearings*].

13. *See* De Vany, Eckert, Meyers, O'Hara & Scott, *A Property System for Market Allocation of the Electromagnetic Spectrum: A Legal-Economic-Engineering Study,* 21 Stan. L. Rev. 1499 (1969); Minasian, *Property Rights in Radiation: An Alternative Approach to Radio Frequency Allocation,* 18 J.L. & Econ. 221 (1975).

14. *See Hearings, supra* note 12, at 79.

15. *See id.* at 81 (testimony of Thomas Krattenmaker referring tangentially to this argument); National Telecommunications and

INFORMATION ADMINISTRATION, 98th CONG., 1ST SESS., PRINT AND ELECTRONIC MEDIA: THE CASE FOR FIRST AMENDMENT PARITY, 56–60 (Comm. Print 1983). Fowler & Brenner, *A Marketplace Approach to Broadcast Regulation,* 60 TEX. L. REV. 207 (1982), argue via the basic counting methodology (comparing daily newspapers and broadcasting outlets) that the market model is preferable for broadcast. They even reply to Thomas Emerson, who argued that one should count printing presses instead of newspapers, by pointing out the difference between individual and mass communication. T. EMERSON, THE SYSTEM OF FREEDOM OF EXPRESSION 225, n.83 (1970).

16. Fowler & Brenner, *supra* note 15.

17. Johnson, *Towers of Babel: The Chaos in Radio Spectrum Utilization and Allocation,* 34 L. & CONTEMP. PROBS. 505, 521–23 (1969).

18. Robinson, *Radio Spectrum Regulation: The Administrative Process and the Problems of Institutional Reform,* 53 MINN. L. REV. 1179, 1253–55 (1969).

19. OFFICE OF TELECOMMUNICATION POLICY, EXECUTIVE OFFICE OF THE PRESIDENT, THE RADIO FREQUENCY SPECTRUM B–2 (1975).

20. For a similar, but not identical suggestion of zoning, see I. POOL, TECHNOLOGIES OF FREEDOM 145 (1983).

21. DBS beams broadcast matter from a satellite in geostationary orbit directly to the ground, over an area as large as the continental U.S. *See* discussion *infra* at 34–36.

22. Berman v. Parker, 348 U.S. 26 (1954). *See also* Poletown Neighborhood Council v. City of Detroit, 410 Mich. 894 (1981) (upholding the condemnation of many tracts of land for the construction of a privately owned assembly plant).

23. *See* Hawaii Housing Auth. v. Midkiff, 104 S.Ct. 2321 (1984).

24. *See* CBS v. Democratic Nat'l Comm., 412 U.S. 94 (1973).

25. In one respect, this should be qualified. Treaties with foreign nations may restrict the extent to which a market may be used. In essence, these treaties may set boundary conditions, or parameters within which a market may operate. The comments in the text are to be taken in this spirit.

CHAPTER 2

1. Such an argument has been made by Nicholas Johnson, in Johnson, *supra* note 17, chap. 1, and is merely an example of the "natural monopoly" rationale for regulation. *See, e.g.,* T. MORGAN, ECONOMIC REGULATION OF BUSINESS 18–20 (1976); and F. SCHERER, INDUSTRIAL MARKET STRUCTURE AND ECONOMIC PERFORMANCE 482 (2d ed. 1980).

2. *See* B. OWEN, ECONOMICS AND FREEDOM OF EXPRESSION 12

(1975). ("There are three stages of production on the supply side for the media marketplace. These are: (1) The creation of messages, (2) the selection or editorial process, and (3) the transmission of messages to the audience. This has more than taxonomic significance, for each stage has different economic characteristics.")

3. *Id.* at 14.

4. "There are two sorts of scale economies. The first we shall call 'first copy' costs. These costs are incurred no matter how large the audience." *Id.* at 16. *See also* Rosse & Dertouzos, *The Evolution of One Newspaper Cities,* in 2 BUREAU OF COMPETITION, FED. TRADE COMM'N, PROCEEDINGS OF THE SYMPOSIUM ON MEDIA CONCENTRATION 429, 439, 441 (1978).

5. B. OWEN, *supra* note 2, at 16 ("The second sort of scale economy is found in the technology of the distribution itself.")

6. *Id.* at 36.

7. Rosse & Dertouzos, *Economic Issues in Mass Communication Industries,* in 1 BUREAU OF COMPETITION, FED. TRADE COMM'N, PROCEEDINGS OF THE SYMPOSIUM ON MEDIA CONCENTRATION 40, 62 (1978).

8. *Id.* at 64 ("The demand for advertising is a function of, among other things, the price of advertising and the number, location and characteristics of readers—other things equal, the demand for advertising will rise when circulation increases.") *See also* B. COMPAIGNE, THE NEWSPAPER INDUSTRY IN THE 1980s: AN ASSESSMENT OF ECONOMICS AND TECHNOLOGY 41 (1980).

9. *Id. See also* B. OWEN, *supra* note 2, at 17 (specialization of demand offsets the scale effects and determines the geographical extent of local newspaper monopolies).

10. *Id.* at 37.

11. *See generally* Rosse & Dertouzos, *supra* note 7, at 72–81 (documents the decline of newspaper competition from 1923 to 1978); Rosse & Dertozous, *supra* note 4, at 429–71.

12. B. OWEN, *supra* note 2, at 48, 51.

13. *Id.* at 48–52.

14. *USA Today,* Fact Sheet (May 22, 1984).

15. *Los Angeles Times,* July 12, 1984, at 1.

16. B. OWEN, *supra* note 2, at 31.

17. *See generally* B. OWEN, *supra* note 2, at 14, 171 (applying umbrella model to both newspaper and magazine industries).

18. *Id.* at 15.

19. Newspapers might wish to avoid the feedback effects on the price of their monopsonistic purchase of content. *Id.* at 15–16. *See generally* J. HENDERSON & R. QUANDT, MICROECONOMIC THEORY 239

(2d ed. 1971) (showing that a monopolist cannot purchase an unlimited quantity of goods at a uniform price).

20. Since the transmission phase is a natural monopoly, there can be only one firm in phase 3. Once that firm vertically integrates, that eliminates all competition in phases 1 and 2 as well. B. OWEN, *supra* note 2, at 48–49; Rosse & Dertouzos, *supra* note 7, at 66, 85.

21. B. OWEN, *supra* note 2, at 169–70; Rosse & Dertouzos, *supra* note 7, at 140.

22. *See* R. NOLL, M. PECK & J. McGOWAN, ECONOMIC ASPECTS OF TELEVISION REGULATION 5 (1973); Rosse & Dertouzos, *supra* note 7, at 92.

23. R. NOLL, M. PECK & J. McGOWAN, *supra* note 22, at 6 (about 100 firms have succeeded in selling a prime-time series to a network in the past few years, and no firm has had more than 20% of the market in any year).

24. Conversation with Charles Jackson of Shooshan and Jackson (January 14, 1985) (member of a leading consulting firm on the economics and engineering of broadcasting, located in Washington, D.C.).

25. *New Television Networks,* in RAND REPORT R. 1408–MF (1973) (cited in B. OWEN, *supra* note 2, at 161).

26. Development of Regulatory Policy in Regard to Direct Broadcast Satellites for the Period Following the 1983 Regional Administrative Radio Conference, 47 C.F.R. §§ 31,555, 31,557 (1982).

27. The same discussion would apply to high-power terrestrial broadcasters. For an expression of skepticism regarding the economic viability of DBS, *see* Anderson, *The Economic, Legal and Scientific Implications of Direct Broadcast Satellites,* 7 COMM. & L. 3 (1985).

28. *See* Note, *Reconciling Red Lion and Tornillo: A Consistent Theory of Media Regulation,* 28 STAN. L. REV. 563, 585–87 (1977).

29. *See* Wirth & Wollert, *The Effects of Market Structure on Television News Pricing,* 28 J. BROADCASTING 215 (1984).

CHAPTER 3

1. Bollinger, *Freedom of the Press and Public Access: Toward a Theory of Partial Regulation of the Mass Media,* 75 U. MICH. L. REV. 1 (1976). *See also* Bollinger, *On the Legal Relationship between Old and New Technologies,* 26 GERMAN YEARBOOK OF INTERNATIONAL LAW 269 (1983).

2. *Id.* at 27, 36–37.

3. *Id.* at 27.

4. *See* 47 U.S.C. § 315.

5. Blasi, *The Checking Value in First Amendment Theory,* 1977 A.B.F. Res. J. 521.

6. Bollinger, *Freedom of the Press, supra* note 1, at 29–31.

7. *Id.* at 32.

8. *Id.* at 37 (emphasis in original).

9. *See generally,* on this distinction, Polsby, *Buckley v. Valeo: The Special Nature of Political Speech,* 1976 Sup. Crt. Rev. 1, 5–14.

10. U.S. Dept. of Commerce, Bureau of the Census, *Statistical Abstract of the United States,* in National Data Book and Guide to Sources 845 (1985).

11. *Id.* at 542, 737.

12. Stone, *Content Regulation and the First Amendment,* 25 Wm. & Mary L. Rev. 189, 217–27 (1983).

13. Shuttlesworth v. Birmingham, 394 U.S. 147 (1969); Cox v. New Hampshire, 312 U.S. 569 (1941) (parade permits).

14. *See* Cornell & Pelcovits, *Access Charges, Costs, and Subsidies: The Effect of Long Distance Competition on Local Rates,* 311–13, in Telecommunications Regulation Today and Tomorrow (Eli Noam ed. 1983).

15. Hearing pursuant to H. R. Res. 803 Before the House Committee on the Judiciary, 93d Cong., 2nd Sess., book V, pt. 1, at 311–20, 346–78; book VIII, at 321–23.

In American Broadcasting and the Licensed First Amendment (unpublished manuscript), Lucas A. Powe, Jr., provides an excellent account of Presidents Roosevelt and Nixon's attempts to control the politics of broadcasters and print publishers by abusing the licensing process for broadcasting. Powe also chronicles the politicization of broadcast regulation under the Eisenhower, Kennedy, Johnson and Carter administrations.

16. *E.g.,* Canby, *The First Amendment Right to Persuade: Access to Radio and Television,* 19 U.C.L.A. L. Rev. 723, 744–46 (1972) (access as a right to a particular channel). For a discussion of access in terms similar to my own, see B. Owen, Economics and Freedom of Expression 21–24 (1975).

17. CBS v. Dem. Nat. Comm., 412 U.S. 94 (1973).

18. *See generally* Canby, *supra* note 16, at 744–46 (concluding that the "right to persuade" is not satisfied by access to a channel with a small audience); J. Barron, Freedom of the Press for Whom? 107–13 (1973) (comparing the audience's right to autonomy and privacy with the speaker's rights); and Nadel, *A Unified Theory of the First Amendment: Divorcing this Medium from the Message,* 11 Ford. Urb. L.J. 163 (1982) (suggesting a common carrier obligation for, inter alia, newspaper and broadcast stations, whenever the publications have substantial economic power).

Individuals' rights of access to the media of mass communications was one of the hottest topics in first amendment scholarship in the 1970s. *See* the review in Polsby, *Candidate Access to the Air: The Uncertain Future of Broadcaster Discretion,* 1981 Sup. Crt. Rev. 223, 224–32.

19. B. Owen, Economics and Freedom of Expression 20–21 (1975). *See generally* Spitzer, *Radio Formats by Administrative Choice,* 47 U. Chi. L. Rev. 647, 652–54 (1980).

20. A whole set of technical assumptions must be satisfied to rigorously prove the statements in the text, but in general they will be correct. *See* sources cited at note 34, *infra.*

21. 581 F.2d 917(D.C.Cir.1978),*cert. denied,*454 U.S.1143 (1982).

22. Cosmopolitan Broadcasting v. FCC, 581 F.2d 917, 919 (D.C. Cir. 1978). This was "mass-appeal" programming in the Newark/New York market.

23. *Id.* at 919 n.2.

24. *Id.* at 921–24.

25. *Id.* at 927.

26. 47 CFR § 73.658(1) (1984).

27. S. Besen, T. Krattenmaker, A. Metzger, Jr. & J. Woodbury, Misregulating Television: Network Dominance and the FCC 86–87 (1984).

28. 85 Duke L.J. 151 (1985).

29. There are political pressures that will interfere with any attempt to fix up the current system by repealing the rules that impede access and diversity. *See* the discussion in text at notes 36–38.

30. This discussion of an enemy's strategies is completely distinct from the possibility that market forces, without the intervention of an enemy, might keep a fringe speaker off the air. *See* text following note 45, *infra.*

31. *See* Lee, *Antitrust Enforcement, Freedom of the Press, and the "Open Market": The Supreme Court on the Structure and Conduct of Mass Media,* 32 Vand. L. Rev. 1249, 1336–37 (1979); and Bennett, *Media Concentration and the FCC: Focusing with a Section Seven Lens,* 66 N.W.L. Rev. 159 (1971).

32. 15 U.S.C. § § 1–11.

33. Fashion Originators' Guild of America v. FTC, 312 U.S. 457 (1941); and Klor's Inc. v. Broadway Hale Stores, Inc. 359 U.S. 207 (1959).

34. *See* the extensive discussion in B. Owen, J. Beebe & W. Manning, Jr., Television Economics, 49–70 (1974); *see also* J. Beebe & B. Owen, Alternative Structures for Television, Office of Telecommunications Policy, Staff Research Paper OTP–SP–10 (1972).

35. B. Owen, J. Beebe & W. Manning, Jr., *supra* note 34, at 49–70.

36. *See* D. GINSBURG, REGULATION OF BROADCASTING 163–68 (1979). 163–68 (1979).

37. For a political/economic description of much FCC decision making that is similar in spirit to mine, *see* R. Cass, REVOLUTION IN THE WASTELAND, 37–55 (1981).

38. Hentoff, *Who Controls TV?* 33 LOOK 27 (No. 13, June 24, 1969); and Smith, *Censorship Veil Falling from Smothers Episode,* Los Angeles Times, Sept. 10, 1969.

39. *See* Dissenting Statement of Commissioner Glen O. Robinson, *The Handling of Public Issues under the Fairness Doctrine and the Public Interest Standards,* 58 F.C.C.2d 691, *rev'd in part* 567 F.2d 1095 (D.C. Cir. 1977), *cert. denied,* 436 U.S. 1095, 98 S.Ct. 2820 (1979) (only 19 out of 4,280 formal fairness complaints in 1973 and 1974 resulted in findings adverse to the licensee).

40. E.g. the equal time provisions under 47 U.S.C. § 315 (1982).

41. In fact, when the FCC attempted to reduce the uncertainty in renewals, they found their task impossible, Formulation of Policies Relating to the Broadcast Renewal Applicant, Stemming From the Comparative Hearing Process, 40 R.R.2d 763 (1977), *aff'd sub nom* National Black Media Coalition v. F.C.C., 589 F.2d 578 (D.C. Cir. 1978); or blocked by the D.C. Circuit, Citizens Communications Center v. FCC, 447 F.2d 1201 (D.C. Cir. 1971).

42. B. OWEN, J. BEEBE & W. MANNING, JR. *supra* note 34, at 172.

43. *See* discussion in text at notes 17–18, *supra.*

44. *See* BARRON, *supra* note 18.

45. *See* Nadel, *supra* note 18, suggesting a right of access to both print and broadcast, on exactly these grounds.

Note that, to the extent a market system does not have the barriers to entry into media markets that are provided in television by the current system, a market system will produce somewhat lower prices for access to television. *See, e.g.,* Wirth & Wollert, *The Effects of Market Structure on Television News Pricing,* 28 J. BROADCASTING 215 (1984) (finding that concentration in broadcasting produces higher prices for spot time on television news).

PART 2

1. Essentially, these rationales provide no justification for greater content control of *radio.* One could create hypotheses for radio that are analogous to the reviewed hypotheses about television. However, there seems to be no research on these hypotheses, and no one even seems to be discussing them.

Although motion pictures are not directly addressed in this book, much of the material on sex and violence seems directly applicable.

2. The persuasiveness of a product advertisement, for example, is often related (though not always positively) to its vividness. Kisielius & Sternthal, *Detecting and Explaining Vividness Effects in Attitudinal Judgments,* 21 J. MARKETING RESEARCH 54 (1984).

Television's presumed capability of delivering a more vivid message than print could form the basis of the distinction between the two media. The normative implications of the phenomenon as related to product marketing and other persuasive discourse, however, are by no means obvious and are beyond the scope of this book. This book also will not address media difference, in such areas as, say, cognitive processing. *See* Pezdek, Lehrer & Simon, *The Relationship Between Reading and Cognitive Processing of Television and Radio,* 55 CHILD DEV. 2072 (1984).

3. For an examination of television's effect on the development of children's reading skills, *see* Roberts, Bachen, Hornby & Hernandez-Ramos, *Reading and Television,* 11 COM. RESEARCH 9 (1984).

CHAPTER 4

1. This rationale is spelled out at great length in very accessible (if not scientific) style, in J. MANDER, FOUR ARGUMENTS FOR THE ELIMINATION OF TELEVISION 157–261 (1978).

2. *See generally* J. BETTMAN, AN INFORMATION PROCESSING THEORY OF CONSUMER CHOICE 89–92 (1978).

3. *See* Krugman, *Memory Without Recall, Exposure Without Perception,* 17 J. ADVERTISING RESEARCH 7 (1977).

4. Krugman & Hartley, *Passive Learning from Television,* 34 PUBLIC OPINION QUARTERLY 184 (1970). Economists have begun to explore the implications of this line of work for the design of trade and consumer regulation. *See* Beales, Mazis, Salop & Staelin, *Consumer Search and Public Policy,* 8 J. CONSUMER RESEARCH 11, 13–15 (1981).

5. Bechtel, Achelpohl & Akers, *Correlates Between Observed Behavior and Questionnaire Responses on Television Viewing,* in 4 NAT'L INST. OF MENTAL HEALTH, U.S. DEP'T OF HEW, TELEVISION AND SOCIAL BEHAVIOR 274 (1972) [entire report hereinafter cited as TELEVISION AND SOCIAL BEHAVIOR]; Ward, *Effects of Television Advertising on Children and Adolescents,* 4 TELEVISION AND SOCIAL BEHAVIOR at 432, 438, (finding children spend 65% of their "viewing" time actually watching programs).

6. Murray, *Television in Inner-City Homes: Viewing Behavior of Young Boys,* in TELEVISION AND SOCIAL BEHAVIOR 345, 356–61 (observing some subjects imitating or otherwise reacting to the viewed program); Robinson, *Toward Defining the Functions of Television,* in

4 TELEVISION AND SOCIAL BEHAVIOR 591–92 (finding an average 38% of the subjects talked during the viewing of a program).

7. Appel, Weinstein & Weinstein, *Brain Activity and Recall of TV Advertising*, 19 J. ADVERTISING RESEARCH 7 (1979).

8. *Id.* at 9.

9. *Id.* at 12–13.

10. Krugman, *Point of View: Sustained Viewing of Television*, 20 J. ADVERTISING RESEARCH 65 (1980).

11. Weinstein, Appel & Weinstein, *Brain Activity Responses to Magazine and Television Advertising*, 20 J. ADVERTISING RESEARCH 57 (1980).

12. *Id.* at 58.

13. *Id.*

14. *Id.* at 59–62.

15. John R. Rossiter in *Point of View: Brain Hemisphere Activity*, 20 J. ADVERTISING RESEARCH 75 (1980), comments on the study by Weinstein, Appel, and Weinstein. Rossiter notes that because the magazine advertisements contained a large amount of *pictorial* matter, and because the television show contained a great deal of auditory *verbal* matter, the study does not provide a clear theoretical test of the left- versus right-brain hypothesis (i.e., the left brain is concerned with verbalization, the right brain with images). However, it seems to me that the Weinstein, Appel, and Weinstein study *does* provide a test of the hypotheses about the relative brain functions of people who read magazines (which usually have some pictures) and who watch television (which usually has some words). Second, Rossiter notes that the subjects were *women,* and that women's brains seem to be less laterally specialized than men's brains. Therefore, the failure to find strong evidence of differential brain function may prove little about male viewers.

16. 11 J. ADVERTISING RESEARCH 3 (1971).

17. *Id.* at 5.

18. F. EMERY & M. EMERY, A CHOICE OF FUTURES (1976). *See generally* Hansen, *Hemispheral Lateralization: Implications for Understanding Consumer Behavior*, 8 J. CONSUMER RESEARCH 23 (1981).

19. *See* Schwartz, *Can Group Differences in Hemispheric Asymmetry be Inferred from Behavioral Laterality Indices?* in 3 BRAIN & COGNITION 57, 62–63 (1984) ("there is no clear consensus about what neurophysiological differences really mean ").

CHAPTER 5

1. This book will attempt no comprehensive definition of "sexually explicit" matter. Where the specific content of a communication

seems to be important, I will explain it. In general, it seems that one must distinguish between depictions of consensual sexual behavior and depictions of forced sex, such as rape.

2. Good introductions to these matters may be found in Nelson, *Pornography and Sexual Aggression,* in THE INFLUENCE OF PORNOGRAPHY ON BEHAVIOR (M. Yaffe & E. Nelson eds. 1982); Malamuth & Donnerstein, *The Effects of Aggressive-Pornographic Mass Media Stimuli,* 15 ADVANCES IN EXPERIMENTAL SOC. PSYCHOLOGY 103 (1982); Malamuth, *Aggression Against Women: Cultural and Individual Causes,* in PORNOGRAPHY AND SEXUAL AGGRESSION (N. Malamuth & E. Donnerstein eds. 1984).

Of course, sexually explicit material may also produce "good" effects. First, it can be quite useful in the treatment of inorgasmic people. *See* H. EYSENCK & D. NIAS, SEX, VIOLENCE AND THE MEDIA, 193–99 (1978). Similarly, such matter could be useful as an aphrodisiac, or as "mere entertainment," for other adults. I will ignore such benefits, in general, and concentrate instead on bad effects.

3. 74 Cal. App. 3d 383, 385 (1977).

4. Jaffee, Malamuth, Feingold & Feshbach, *Sexual Arousal and Behavioral Aggression,* 30 J. PERSONALITY & SOC. PSYCHOLOGY 759, 763 (1974).

5. *Id.*

6. *Id. See* Nelson, *supra* note 2, at 183–87 (relating conditioning to *arousal,* which in turn can be related to aggression).

7. Zillmann, Hoyt & Day, *Strength and Duration of the Effect of Aggressive, Violent, and Erotic Communication on Subsequent Aggressive Behavior,* 1 COM. RESEARCH 286, 288–89 (1974).

8. Donnerstein & Hallam, *Facilitating Effects of Erotica on Aggression Against Females,* 36 J. PERSONALITY & SOC. PSYCHOLOGY 1270, 1275–76 (1978).

9. Mosher & Katz, *Pornographic Films, Male Verbal Aggression Against Women, and Guilt,* in 8 TECHNICAL REPORT OF THE COMMISSION ON OBSCENITY AND PORNOGRAPHY 357 (1971) [entire report hereinafter cited as 1971 COMMISSION].

10. *Id;* Nelson, *supra* note 2, at 179–80.

11. A synthesis of two studies produces this theory: Malamuth & Check, *The Effects of Mass Media Exposure on Acceptance of Violence Against Women: A Field Experiment,* 15 J. RESEARCH PERSONALITY 436 (1981); Nelson, *supra* note 2.

12. To the extent that experimental results differ with respect to the medium used, the question remains as to whether these results can be *externalized* (i.e. generalized to the "real world"). The resolution of this question is irrelevant for the purposes of this book, as long as it is resolved in the same way for print experiments and broadcast

experiments. *See generally* Krattenmaker & Powe, *Televised Violence: First Amendment Principles and Social Science Theory,* 64 VA. L. REV. 1123, 1147–57 (1978).

For a defense of experimental measurement of the effects of media, see Berkowitz & Donnerstein, *External Validity Is More than Skin Deep: Some Answers to Criticisms of Laboratory Experiments,* 37 AM. PSYCHOLOGIST 245, 247–48, 255 (1982).

Empirical data reviewed are offered only to address the question whether, given that it is possible to measure such behavioral effects at all, there is some measured difference between the media. James Q. Wilson believes that empiricism in this area is useless. *See* Wilson, *Violence, Pornography and Social Science,* 22 PUB. INTEREST 45 (1971).

13. *See generally,* Nelson *supra* note 2, at 176–77.

14. Murphy, Krisak, Stalgaitis & Anderson, *The Use of Penile Tumescence Measures with Incarcerated Rapists: Further Validity Issues,* 13 ARCHIVES SEXUAL BEHAVIOR 545 (1984).

15. Although the Presidential Commission on Obscenity and Pornography's *Report of the Commission on Obscenity and Pornography* (1970) concluded that there was no demonstrable link between pornography and subsequent aggression, subsequent experimental work by Mosher and Katz, *supra* note 9, suggest exactly the opposite. It should be noted that rejection of the commission's findings has been a basis for the regulation of pornography by the FCC and the courts. Dienstbier, *Sex and Violence: Can Research Have It Both Ways?,* 27 J. COM. 176, 178 (1977).

16. Almost all of the work reviewed here involved only one or two exposures to the stimulus. Very recent work suggests that repeated exposure to sexually explicit matter may reduce sexual arousal to erotica that incorporates rape stories, but also induce more callous attitudes toward women and a reduction in repulsion to "deviant" stimuli. *See* Zillmann & Bryant, *Effects of Massive Exposure to Pornography,* in PORNOGRAPHY AND SEXUAL AGGRESSION (Malamuth and Donnerstein eds., 1984); and Ceniti & Malamuth, *Effects of Repeated Exposure to Sexually Violent or Nonviolent Stimuli on Sexual Arousal to Rape and Nonrape Depictions,* 22 BEHAV. RESEARCH AND THERAPY, 535 (1984).

In addition, recent work suggests that *individual* differences between men, which correlate highly with the man's belief in "rape myths," and the man's sexual arousal when viewing rape depictions, can predict willingness to aggress toward women. *See* Malamuth & Check, *Sexual Arousal to Rape Depictions: Individual Differences,* 92 J. ABNORMAL PSYCHOLOGY 55 (1983); Malamuth, *Factors Associated with Rape as Predictors of Laboratory Aggression Against Women,* 45 J. PERSONALITY AND SOC. PSYCHOLOGY 432 (1983); and discussion, *supra* at 83–84.

17. Donnerstein, *Aggressive Erotica and Violence Against Women,* 39 J. PERSONALITY & SOC. PSYCHOLOGY 269 (1980).

18. *Id.* at 272.

19. *Id.* at 274–75.

20. 36 J. PERSONALITY & SOC. PSYCHOLOGY 180 (1978).

21. Donnerstein & Hallam, *supra* note 8.

22. *Id.* at 1272.

23. *Id.*

24. *Id.*

25. *See generally* Nevid, *Exposure to Homoerotic Stimuli: Effects on Attitudes and Affects of Heterosexual Viewers,* 119 J. SOC. PSYCHOLOGY 249 (1983).

26. Zillmann, Hoyt & Day, *supra* note 7.

27. *Id.* at 298.

28. 17 J. EXPERIMENTAL SOC. PSYCHOLOGY 31 (1981).

29. 128 AM. J. PSYCHOLOGY 67 (1971).

30. Zillmann & Bryant, *supra* note 16.

31. Malamuth & Check, *supra* note 11. For experimental evidence in accord *see* Malamuth & Check, *The Effects of Aggressive Pornography on Beliefs in Rape Myths: Individual Differences,* 19 J. RES. PERSONALITY 299 (1985).

32. Malamuth & Check, *supra* note 11, at 439.

33. On a scale from 1 ("strongly disagree") to 7 ("strongly agree"). *Id.*

34. *Id.*

35. *Id.*

36. Malamuth, *Rape Proclivity Among Males,* 37 J. SOC. ISSUES 138, 142 (1981); Scully & Marolla, *Convicted Rapists' Vocabulary of Motive: Excuses and Justifications,* 31 SOC. PROBS. 530 (1984).

37. Burt, *Cultural Myths and Supports for Rape,* 38 J. PERSONALITY & SOC. PSYCHOLOGY 217, (1980).

38. Zillmann & Bryant, *supra* note 16.

39. Donnerstein & Berkowitz, *Victim Reactions in Aggressive Erotic Films as a Factor in Violence Against Women,* 41 J. PERSONALITY & SOC. PSYCHOLOGY 710 (1981).

40. *Id.* at 717. There is some parallel for these results in studies of *violent* programming. Viewers' perceptions of violence tend to vary with the outcomes portrayed for victims of filmed or televised violence. *See* Gunter, *Personality and Perceptions of Harmful and Harmless TV Violence,* 4 PERSONALITY & INDIVIDUAL DIFFERENCES 665 (1983).

41. Malamuth & Check, *supra* note 11, at 443. One study used a slide show accompanied by an audio presentation that could be considered similar, although not identical, to television. This study found that depictions of rape can produce substantial sexual arousal in college-age male subjects, and that subsequent sexual fantasizing by the subjects may have more violent, coercive content because of such depictions. Malamuth, *Rape Fantasies as a Function of Exposure to Violent Sexual Stimuli,* 10 ARCHIVES SEXUAL BEHAV. 33 (1981).

42. Informing subjects that they had ingested alcohol, regardless of whether or not they had actually done so, apparently disinhibited male arousal to depictions of rape. *See* Briddell, Rimm, Caddy, Krawitz, Sholis & Wunderlin, *Effects of Alcohol and Cognitive Set on Sexual Arousal to Deviant Stimuli,* 87 J. ABNORMAL PSYCHOLOGY 418 (1978). *See also* Zillmann & Bryant, *Pornography, Sexual Callousness, and the Trivialization of Rape,* 32 J. COM. 10 (1982).

43. *See* Donnerstein, Donnerstein & Evans, *Erotic Stimuli and Aggression: Facilitation or Inhibition,* 32 J. PERSONALITY & SOC. PSYCHOLOGY 237 (1975).

44. Zillmann, Hoyt & Day, *supra* note 7.

45. Ramirez, Zillmann & Bryant, *Effects of Erotica on Retaliatory Behavior as a Function of Level of Prior Provocation,* 43 J. PERSONALITY & SOC. PSYCHOLOGY 971, 977 (1982).

46. Malamuth, Heim & Feshbach, *Sexual Responsiveness of College Students to Rape Depictions: Inhibitory and Disinhibitory Effects,* 38 J. PERSONALITY & SOC. PSYCHOLOGY 399 (1980).

47. *Id.* at 401 (emphasis in original).

48. *Id.* at 404.

49. *Id.* at 406.

50. Malamuth & Check, *Sexual Arousal to Rape and Consenting Depictions: The Importance of the Woman's Arousal,* 89 J. ABNORMAL PSYCHOLOGY 763 (1980).

51. 10 J. APPLIED SOC. PSYCHOLOGY 528 (1980).

52. Jaffe, Malamuth, Feingold & Feshbach, *supra* note 4.

53. *Id.* at 760.

54. 14 J. RESEARCH PERSONALITY 121 (1980).

55. *Id.* at 124.

56. 30 J. PERSONALITY & SOC. PSYCHOLOGY 318, 320 (1974).

57. *See* Nelson, *supra* note 2, at 195, and sources cited therein.

58. Baron & Bell, *Sexual Arousal and Aggression by Males: Effects of Type of Erotic Stimuli and Prior Provocation,* 35 J. PERSONALITY & SOC. PSYCHOLOGY 79 (1977).

59. Compare these results with those obtained with erotic films by Zillmann, Hoyt & Day, *supra* note 7.

60. Jaffe, Malamuth, Feingold & Feshbach, *supra* note 4.

61. Baron & Bell, *supra* note 58, at 85.

62. *See* Malamuth, *supra* note 36, at 145–46. Essentially all experimental work deals with arousal to stimuli and attempts by therapists to reorient sexual offenders' tastes and preferences. *See* sources cited in Nelson, *supra* note 2, at 186–87.

See also Cook & Fosen, *Pornography and the Sex Offender,* in 7 1971 COMMISSION, *supra* note 9, at 149 (finding no difference between sex offenders' and criminal code offenders' arousal in response to a slide show of sexual behavior); Kolarsky, Madlafousek & Novotna, *Stimuli Eliciting Sexual Arousal in Males Who Offend Adult Women: An Experimental Study,* 7 ARCHIVES OF SOC. BEHAVIOR 79 (1978) (male sex offenders, primarily exhibitionists, showed arousal levels comparable to those of normal men when presented with a film of a nude actress acting seductively); Walker, *Erotic Stimuli and the Aggressive Sexual Offender,* in 7 1971 COMMISSION, *supra* note 9, at 91 (generating very little usable data from rapists viewing sexually explicit still photographs, and concluding that the data prove little or nothing).

Differences have been reported, however, in sexual arousal between subjects possessing a high "psychoticism" quotient and those who do not. Those viewers with a high psychoticism quotient (measuring perhaps a lack of "welfare emotions"—joy, love, and pride) were more aroused by rape depictions than by nonrape depictions, whereas the opposite was true for viewers with a low psychoticism quotient. Barnes, Malamuth & Check, *Psychoticism and Sexual Arousal to Rape Depictions,* 5 PERSONALITY AND INDIVIDUAL DIFFERENCES 273 (1984) (measuring responses to *auditory* depictions).

63. *See* Rapaport & Burkhart, *Personality and Attitudinal Characteristics of Sexually Coercive College Males,* 93 J. ABNORMAL PSYCHOLOGY 216, 219 (1984) (15% of 201 college males surveyed had intercourse with a woman "against her will").

64. Malamuth, *supra* note 36, at 140.

65. *Supra* note 16.

66. *See* Ben-Veniste, *infra* note 70; Kupperstein & Wilson, *infra* note 70. To the extent that the different media are mentioned, the availability of print and audiovisual materials appears to correlate very highly, precluding separation of their effects.

67. *See generally* Nelson, *supra* note 2, at 212–13.

68. J. SEX RESEARCH, 226, 234–35 (1980).

69. Act of May 12, 1975, ch. 71, 1975 Cal. Stat. 131 (codified as amended at CAL. EVID. CODE §§ 972, 985, and in scattered sections of CAL. PENAL CODE.) *See generally,* Kutschinsky, *Towards an Explanation of the Decrease in Registered Sex Crimes in Copenhagen,* in 3 1971 COMMISSION, *supra* note 9, at 263.

70. *Compare, id.* (finding that for certain minor offenses—

exhibitionism and peeping—increased availability of pornography *reduces* the offense rate); Ben-Veniste, *Pornography and Sex Crime,* in 7 1971 COMMISSION, *supra* note 9, at 245 (finding that increased availability of pornography caused no increase in the rate of sex crime); Kupperstein & Wilson, *Erotica and Antisocial Behavior,* in 7 1971 COMMISSION, *supra* note 9, at 311 (finding that data cannot prove or disprove a link between the increased availability of pornography in the U.S. in the 1960s and the large increase in sex crimes and illegitimate births) *with* Court, *Pornography and Sex Crimes: A Re-evaluation in the Light of Recent Trends Around the World,* 5 INT'L J. CRIMINOLOGY & PENOLOGY 129 (1976) (finding likely a positive correlation between pornography and sex crimes—particularly forcible rape).

71. *See* Michael and Zumpe, *Annual Rhythms in Human Violence and Sexual Aggression in the United States and the Role of Temperature,* 30 SOC. BIOLOGY 263 (1983).

72. 1971 COMMISSION, *supra* note 9, at 1.

73. Walker, *supra* note 62, concludes that rapists encounter less pornographic material than do normals, but employs questions that lump all media types together. Cook & Fosen, *Pornography and the Sex Offender,* in 7 1971 COMMISSION, *supra* note 9, at 149, conclude that convicted sex offenders have less experience with pornography than do prisoners who have been convicted of non–sex-related crimes, but they construct a composite "severity frequency score" that combines all media. Davis & Braucht, *Exposure to Pornography, Character, and Sexual Deviance,* in 7 1971 COMMISSION, *supra* note 9, at 173, present only summary statistics of exposure to pornography that fail to differentiate between the media.

74. 7 1971 COMMISSION *supra* note 9, at 163.

75. In addition, the available studies have reached opposite conclusions on whether sex deviants tend to have more or less exposure to pornography. *See generally* Nelson, *supra* note 2, at 214–15.

CHAPTER 6

1. *See* Krattenmaker & Powe, *supra* note 12, chap. 5.

2. These are the Dodd hearings in 1961, the Kefauver hearings in 1954, and the Pastore hearings in 1972. *See* Krattenmaker & Powe, *supra* note 12, chap. 5, at 1125–34, and R. LIEBERT, J. SPRAFKIN & E. DAVIDSON, THE EARLY WINDOW 47–100 (2d ed. 1978) for the political background on these hearings.

3. *See* R. LIEBERT, J. SPRAFKIN & E. DAVIDSON, *supra* note 2. For some of the most recent installments on this issue, see Weitzer & Lometti, *Researching Television Violence,* 21 SOCIETY 22 (1984), and

Chaffee, Gerbner, Hamburg, Pierce, Rubinstein, Sergal & Singer, *Defending the Indefensible,* 21 SOCIETY 30 (1984). Recently, the National Coalition on Television Violence has asked the FTC to require warnings before the "Dungeons and Dragons" cartoon show, a violent fantasy show that petitioners allege has "deadly effect." See *FTC Asked to Require Warnings Before TV Show,* BROADCASTING, Jan. 28, 1985, at 88.

4. Indeed, R. LEIBERT, J. SPRAFKIN & E. DAVIDSON, *supra* note 2; H. EYSENCK & D. NIAS, *supra* note 2, chap. 5; and Krattenmaker and Powe, *Televised Violence: First Amendment Principles and Social Science Theory,* 64 VA. L. REV. 1123 (1978) provide extensive reviews of the literature on the violence hypothesis without giving any extended treatment to this normative point.

5. *See* Krattenmaker and Powe, *supra* note 4; R. LIEBERT, J. SPRAFKIN & E. DAVIDSON, *supra* note 2; H. EYSENCK AND D. NIAS, *supra* note 2, chap. 5; Geen, *Aggression and Television Violence,* in 2 AGGRESSION, THEORETICAL AND EMPIRICAL REVIEW 103 (1983); Kaplan & Singer, *Television Violence and Viewer Aggression: A Reexamination of the Evidence,* 32 J. SOC. ISSUES 35 (1976).

6. Consider also the "Born Innocent" program, discussed in text at p. 74. *See generally* Berkowitz, *The Contagion of Violence: An S-R Mediational Analysis of Some Effects of Observed Aggression,* 18 NEBRASKA SYMP. ON MOTIVATION 95, 97–99, 101 (1970).

7. One exception, an experiment searching for cognitive effects, which is *not* the subject of this book, is Bailyn, *Mass Media and Children: A Study of Exposure Habits and Cognitive Effects,* 73 PSYCHOLOGICAL MONOGRAPHS 1 (1959). *See also* D. HOWITT & G. CUMBERBATH, MASS MEDIA VIOLENCE AND SOCIETY 96–116 (1975) (explaining differences in findings of studies of different media.)

8. There are a few studies of radio and its effect on aggression, but they do not suggest enough concern to justify discussion. *See* Riccuiti, *Children and Radio: A Study of Listeners and Non-Listeners to Various Types of Radio Programs in Terms of Selected Ability, Attitude, and Behavior Measures,* 44 GENETIC PSYCHOLOGY MONOGRAPH 69 (1951). Further, radio is a dead political issue, as compared to television.

9. *See* Feshbach, *The Catharsis Hypothesis, Aggressive Drive, and the Reduction of Aggression,* 10 AGGRESSIVE BEHAVIOR 91 (1984) (the most recent survey and analysis of the problems with catharsis theory); Feshbach, *The Stimulating Versus Cathartic Effects of a Vicarious Aggressive Activity,* 63 J. ABNORMAL & SOC. PSYCHOLOGY 381 (1961); Feshbach, *The Drive-Reducing Function of Fantasy Behavior,* 50 J. ABNORMAL & SOC. PSYCHOLOGY 3 (1955).

10. *See* H. EYSENCK & D. NIAS, *supra* note 2, chap. 5, at 55.

11. *See* Bandura, Ross & Ross, *Transmission of Aggression Through Imitation of Aggressive Models,* 63 J. ABNORMAL PSYCHOLOGY 575 (1961).

12. *See* F. WERTHAM, SEDUCTION OF THE INNOCENT 84–118 (1954).

13. *See* Huesmann, *Television Violence and Aggressive Behavior,* in National Institute of Mental Health, 2 TELEVISION AND BEHAVIOR: TEN YEARS OF SCIENTIFIC PROGRESS AND IMPLICATIONS FOR THE EIGHTIES (1982) at 126, 133–34 [entire report cited hereinafter as TELEVISION AND BEHAVIOR].

14. *See, e.g.,* A. BANDURA, AGGRESSION (1973); Bandura & Huston, *Identification as a Process of Incidental Learning,* 63 J. ABNORMAL SOC. PSYCHOLOGY 311 (1961); Bandura, Ross & Ross, *supra* note 11.

15. Bandura, Ross & Ross, *Imitation of Film-mediated Aggressive Models,* 66 J. ABNORMAL SOC. PSYCHOLOGY 3 (1963).

16. *Id.* at 4–5.

17. Bandura, Ross & Ross, *supra* note 15, at 5.

18. *Id.*

19. *Id.* at 6.

20. *Id.* at 6–7.

21. *See* R. LIEBERT, J. SPRAFKIN & E. DAVIDSON, *supra* note 2, at 58–59.

22. Hanratty, Liebert, Morris & Fernandez, *Imitation of Film Mediated Aggression Against Live and Inanimate Objects,* 4 AM. PSYCHOLOGICAL A. PROC. 457 (1969); Hanratty, O'Neal & Sulzer, *Effect of Frustration Upon Imitation of Aggression,* 21 J. PERSONALITY & SOC. PSYCHOLOGY 30 (1972) (finding aggression in 30 boys aged 6–7 years old only when they were frustrated); Savitsky, Rogers, Izard & Liebert, *Role of Frustration and Anger in the Imitation of Filmed Aggression Against a Human Victim,* 29 PSYCHOLOGICAL REPORTS 807 (1971). *See also* Bandura, Ross & Ross, *supra* note 11; Lövaas, *Effect of Exposure to Symbolic Aggression on Aggressive Behavior,* 32 CHILD DEV. 37 (1961).

23. *See supra* authorities cited in note 22. Experimenters have also recorded increased levels of aggression in children who are trying to allocate the right to see a "peep show" among themselves. *See* Hapkiewicz & Roden, *The Effect of Aggressive Cartoons on Children's Interpersonal Play,* 42 CHILD DEV. 1583 (1971). The most recent example of this work is Day & Ghandour, *The Effect of Television-Mediated and Real-Life Aggression on the Behavior of Lebanese Children,* 38 J. EXP. CHILD. PSYCH. 7 (1984), in which the author interprets the data to support Bandura's modeling theory despite numerous null findings in the statistical tests of the data. *See* table 2, *id.* at 13.

24. *See supra* note 14, chap. 5 and accompanying text.

25. Berkowitz & Geen, *Stimulus Qualities of the Target of Aggression: A Further Study,* 5 J. PERSONALITY & SOC. PSYCHOLOGY 364 (1967); Berkowitz & Geen, *Film Violence and the Cue Properties of Available Targets,* 3 J. PERSONALITY & SOC. PSYCHOLOGY 525 (1966); Geen and Berkowitz, *Some Conditions Facilitating the Occurrence of Aggression after the Observation of Violence,* 35 J. PERSONALITY 666 (1967); Geen & Berkowitz, *Name-mediated Aggressive Cue Properties,* 34 J. PERSONALITY 456 (1966); Walters & Thomas, *Enhancement of Punitiveness by Visual and Audiovisual Displays,* 17 CAN. J. PSYCHOLOGY 244 (1963).

26. "The Untouchables" was an extremely violent and extremely popular television show.

27. Liebert & Baron, *Short Term Effects of Televised Aggression on Children's Aggressive Behavior,* in 2 TELEVISION AND SOCIAL BEHAVIOR, *supra* note 5, chap. 4, at 181, 185.

28. Hartmann, *Influence of Symbolically Modeled Instrumental Aggression and Pain Cues on Aggressive Behavior,* 11 J. PERSONALITY AND SOC. PSYCHOLOGY 280 (1969). *See also* Shemberg, Leventhal & Allman, *Aggression Machine Performance and Rated Aggression,* 3 J. EXPERIMENTAL RESEARCH PERSONALITY 117 (1968) (finding that children who rated higher in aggression according to two counselors who knew them well also scored as more aggressive on a Buss machine).

29. H. EYSENCK & D. NIAS, *supra* note 2, chap. 5, at 154 (citing West, Berkowitz, Sebastian   & Parke, The Effect of Viewing Physical Aggression on Verbal Aggression in Delinquent Girls (1975) (unpublished manuscript).

30. Hicks, *Imitation and Retention of Film-mediated Aggressive Peer and Adult Models,* 2 J. PERSONALITY & SOC. PSYCHOLOGY 97 (1965); Kniveton, *The Effect of Rehearsal Delay on Long-Term Imitation of Filmed Aggression,* 64 BRIT. J. PSYCHOLOGY 259 (1973). Researchers have also found some evidence that television violence may produce a type of numbing effect, producing children who are less sensitive to violence. *See* Rabinovitch, McLean, Markham & Talbott, *Children's Violence Perception as a Function of Television Violence,* in 5 TELEVISION AND SOCIAL BEHAVIOR, *supra* note 5, chap. 4, at 231 (providing ambiguous support for this proposition).

31. *See* Lövaas, *supra* note 22. Mussen & Rutherford, *Effects of Aggressive Cartoons on Children's Aggressive Play,* 62 J. ABNORMAL & SOC. PSYCHOLOGY 461 (1961). *But see* Siegal, *Film-Mediated Fantasy Aggression and Strength of Aggressive Drive,* 27 CHILD DEV. 365 (1956) (finding a statistically insignificant greater amount of aggressive behavior with children watching the "aggressive" cartoon).

See also Hapkiewicz & Roden, *supra* note 23 (finding no statistically meaningful difference in aggressive behavior between those children who viewed the "aggressive" cartoon and those who did not, but finding a lesser willingness to share among the first group).

32. Berkowitz & Geen, *Film Violence and the Cue Properties of Available Targets*, 3 J. PERSONALITY & SOC. PSYCHOLOGY 525 (1966). *See also* Swart & Berkowitz, *Effects of a Stimulus Associated with a Victim's Pain on Later Aggression*, 33 J. PERSONALITY & SOC. PSYCHOLOGY 623 (1976) (regarding conditioning).

33. Bandura, *Influence of Model's Reinforcement Contingencies on the Acquisition of Imitative Responses*, 1 J. PERSONALITY & SOC. PSYCHOLOGY 589, 590 (1965).

34. *See supra* note 15 and accompanying text.

35. Bandura, *supra* note 33, at 591.

36. Berkowitz, *Some Aspects of Observed Aggression*, 2 J. PERSONALITY & SOC. PSYCHOLOGY 359 (1965); Hoyt, *Effect of Media Violence "Justification" on Aggression*, 14 J. BROADCASTING 455 (1970); Meyer, *Effects of Viewing Justified and Unjustified Real Film Violence on Aggressive Behavior*, 23 J. PERSONALITY & SOC. PSYCHOLOGY 21 (1972). *See also* Geen, *Behavioral and Physiological Reactions to Observed Violence: Effects of Prior Exposure to Aggressive Stimuli*, 40 J. PERSONALITY & SOC. PSYCHOLOGY 868 (1981).

37. Leifer & Roberts, *Children's Responses to Television Violence*, in 2 TELEVISION AND SOCIAL BEHAVIOR, *supra* note 5, chap. 4, at 43.

The nature of an audience with which a young (5–6 years old) child views a film may also produce effects upon aggression. *See* Leyens, Herman and Durand, *The Influence of an Audience Upon the Reactions to Filmed Violence*, 12 EUR. J. SOC. PSYCHOLOGY 131 (1982).

38. Tan & Scruggs, *Does Exposure to Comic Book Violence Lead to Aggression in Children?*, 57 JOURNALISM Q. 579 (1980).

39. *Id.* at 581. Examples taken from Liefer & Roberts, *supra* note 37, at 131–32.

40. Tan & Scruggs, *supra* note 38, at 583.

41. Berkowitz, *supra* note 6, at 110–11.

42. Fisher & Harris, *Modeling, Arousal, and Aggression*, 100 J. SOC. PSYCHOLOGY 219 (1976).

43. *Id.* at 224, 225 (admitting that their "inhibition" theory of these results needs "further theorizing and research" to "ascertain the parameters of such inhibition.")

44. Spiegler & Weiland, *The Effects of Written Vicarious Consequences on Observers' Willingness to Imitate and Ability to Recall Modeling Cues*, 44 J. PERSONALITY 260 (1976).

45. Weiland, *Acceptance and Recall of Written Prosocial, Neutral, and Aggressive Modeling Cues,* 49 J. PERSONALITY 161 (1981).

46. *See supra* text accompanying notes 15–20.

47. *See* Weiland, *supra* note 45.

48. *See* Leifer & Roberts, *Responses to Television Violence,* in 2 TELEVISION AND SOCIAL BEHAVIOR, *supra* note 5, chap. 4, at 43.

49. CODE OF THE COMICS MAGAZINE ASSOCIATION OF AMERICA (1954) (reprinted in R. REITBERGER & W. FUCHS, COMICS, ANATOMY OF A MASS MEDIUM 248 (1971) [hereinafter cited as COMICS CODE].

50. S. FESHBACH & R. SINGER, TELEVISION AND AGGRESSION (1971).

51. H. EYSENCK & D. NIAS, *supra* note 2, chap. 5, at 126.

52. *Id.*

53. Krattenmaker & Powe, *supra* note 4, at 1143.

54. H. EYSENCK & D. NIAS, *supra* note 2, chap. 5, at 126; R. LIEBERT, J. SPRAFKIN & E. DAVIDSON, *supra* note 2, at 65–66.

55. H. EYSENCK & D. NIAS, *supra* note 2, chap. 5, at 126–27.

56. *See* Leyens, Parke, Camino & Berkowitz, *Effects of Movie Violence on Aggression in a Field Setting as a Function of Group Dominance and Cohesion,* 32 J. PERSONALITY & SOC. PSYCHOLOGY 346 (1975); Parke, Berkowitz, Leyens, West & Sebastian, *Some Effects of Violent and Nonviolent Movies on the Behavior of Juvenile Delinquents,* 10 ADVANCES EXPERIMENTAL SOC. PSYCHOLOGY 135 (1977); Steuer, Applefield & Smith, *Televised Aggression and the Interpersonal Aggression of Preschool Children,* 11 J. EXPERIMENTAL CHILD PSYCHOLOGY 442 (1971) (later experiments, however, used only 5 pairs of matched subjects). *See also* Krattenmaker & Powe, *supra* note 4, at 1143 citing W. Wells, Television and Aggression: A Replication of an Experimental Field Study (1972) (unpublished manuscript) (producing results "dissimilar" to Feshbach & Singer); H. EYSENCK & D. NIAS, *supra* note 2, chap. 5, at 128–29 (citing the Wells Study as supporting the violence hypothesis for physical aggression and as supporting the catharsis hypothesis for verbal aggression and as being plagued by observer bias).

57. *See* Stein & Friedrich, *Prosocial Television and Young Children—Effects of Verbal Labeling and Role Playing on Learning and Behavior,* 46 CHILD DEVELOPMENT 27 (1975). Stein and Friedrich included "verbalization of feeling," such as "I hate you," as a prosocial act, whereas other experimenters often classify such statements as aggression. *Id.* at 81; Parke, Berkowitz, Leyens, West & Sebastian, *supra* note 56, at 141 (citing Sawin, Aggressive Behavior Among Children in Small Playgroup Settings with Violent Television (1973) (unpublished doctoral dissertation) (unseen by this author);

S. MILGRAM & R. SHOTLAND, TELEVISION AND ANTISOCIAL BEHAVIOR: FIELD EXPERIMENTS (1973) (using episodes of "Medical Center," a real television show). The Milgram and Shotland work, funded by the CBS network, has been described as having "many flaws" by R. LIEBERT, J. SPRAFKIN & E. DAVIDSON, *supra* note 2, at 115, who are strong advocates of the violence hypothesis, and as "the most imaginative research yet undertaken in a natural setting" by Krattenmaker & Powe, *supra* note 12, chap. 5, at 1149, who are far more skeptical.

See also R. LIEBERT, J. SPRAFKIN & E. DAVIDSON, *supra* note 2, at 122 (discussing de Konig, Conradie &   Nell, The Effect of Different Kinds of Television Programming on the Youth, Pretoria, Republic of South Africa: Human Sciences Research Council, Dept. No. Comm. 20 (1980) (unseen by this author).

58. *See* Freedman, *Effect of Television Violence on Aggression,* 96 PSYCHOLOGICAL BULL. 227, 227–35 (1984) (reviewing television field studies and finding "only the slightest encouragement for the causal hypothesis," at 234, and generally appraising the literature in a fashion similar to mine).

59. W. BELSON, TELEVISION VIOLENCE AND THE ADOLESCENT BOY (1978). Belson gathered his data on television diet by asking the subjects and their parents. Recent work suggests that parents tend to overestimate children's viewing. *See* Anderson, Field, Collins, Lorch & Nathan, *Estimates of Young Children's Time with Television: A Methodological Comparison of Parent Reports with Time Lapse Video Home Observation,* 56 CHILD DEVELOPMENT 1345 (1985).

60. For a full description of his methodology, *see id.* at 60–92. There is also some experimental work confirming the reverse violence hypothesis. *See* Fenigstein, *Does Aggression Cause a Preference for Viewing Media Violence,* 37 J. PERS. & SOCIAL PSYCH. 2307 (1979).

61. Belson tested many, many hypotheses. *See* W. BELSON, *supra* note 59, at 14–17, 24–60. Yet, it will avail us little to explore them all.

62. *Id.* at 15 (emphasis in original).

63. *Id.* at 253, 366.

64. *Id.* at 15.

65. *Id.* at 403 (emphasis in original).

66. *Id.* at 408–09.

67. *Id.* at 409.

68. *Id.* (emphasis in original).

69. *See* Andison, *TV Violence and Viewer Aggression: A Cumulation of Study Results 1956–76,* 41 PUB. OPIN. Q. 314 (1977). Field work has recently analyzed the relationship between video games and aggression. The results are similar to those obtained for television. *See* Dominick, *Videogames, Television Violence, and Aggression in Teenagers,* 34 J. COM. 137 (1984).

70. The largest of the studies clearly supporting the violence hypothesis is Belson's, *supra* note 59. Others would include McLeod, Atkin & Chaffee, *Adolescents, Parents and Television Use: Self-Report and Other-Report Measures from the Wisconsin Sample*, in 3 TELEVISION AND SOCIAL BEHAVIOR, *supra* note 5, chap. 4, at 239, which found a positive correlation between violence viewing and various self-reported measures of aggressive behavior). *See also* Greenberg, *British Children and Televised Violence*, 38 PUB. OPINION Q. 531 (1974); McIntyre & Teevan, *Television Violence and Deviant Behavior*, in 3 TELEVISION AND SOCIAL BEHAVIOR, *supra* note 5, chap. 4, at 383; Robinson & Bachman, *Television Viewing Habits and Aggression*, in 3 TELEVISION AND SOCIAL BEHAVIOR, *supra* note 5, chap. 4, at 372.

A few studies could plausibly be regarded as supporting both the null hypothesis and the violence hypothesis. H. HIMMELWEIT, A. OPPENHEIM & P. VINCE, TELEVISION AND THE CHILD (1958); Hartnagel, Teevan & McIntyre, *Television Violence and Violent Behavior*, 54 SOC. FORCES 341 (1975).

A very few support the null hypothesis. *See, e.g.,* Balon, *TV Viewing Preferences as Correlates of Adult Dysfunctional Behavior*, 55 JOURNALISM Q. 288 (1978) (using prison inmates as subjects). *See generally* Andison, *supra* note 69.

71. *See* Balon, *supra* note 70, at 537–41, discussing the phenomenon.

72. Eron, Lefkowitz, Huesmann & Walder, *Does Television Violence Cause Aggression?*, 27 AM. PSYCHOLOGIST 253 (1972).

73. *Id.* at 254. There has been a great deal of debate over the validity of these results. *See* Huesmann, Eron, Lefkowitz & Walder, *Television Violence and Aggression: The Causal Effect Remains*, 28 AM. PSYCHOLOGIST 617 (1973).

74. *See* Eron & Huesmann, *Adolescent Aggression and Television*, 347 ANNALS N.Y. ACAD. OF SCI. 319 (1980) (reporting data collected over a three-year period in Oak Park and Chicago, Ill. The violence hypothesis for girls, however, was not confirmed by this study); Fraczek, *Age and Gender Related Trends in Patterns of TV Violence Viewing and Interpersonal Aggression in Children*, 14 POL. PRESIDENTIAL BULL. 25 (1983) (violence hypothesis confirmed with a sample of 237 Warsaw children viewing Polish television in a three-year longitudinal study); Huesmann, Lagerspetz & Eron, *Intervening Variable in the TV Violence–Aggression Relation: Evidence from Two Countries*, 20 DEV. PSYCH. 746, 757 (1984); Singer & Singer, *Television Viewing and Aggressive Behavior in Preschool Children: A Field Study*, 347 ANNALS N.Y. ACAD. OF SCI. 289 (1980); Eron & Huesmann, *Television Violence and Aggressive Behavior*, 7 ADVANCES IN CLINICAL CHILD PSYCHOLOGY 35 (1984).

75. Milavsky, Kessler, Stipp & Rubens, *Television and Aggression: The Results of a Panel Study,* in 2 TELEVISION AND BEHAVIOR, *supra* note 13, at 138, 155 (finding "no signficant association between violent television exposure and subsequent change in aggression.") This study, which was funded by the NBC television network, has been the focus of some controversy. *See Disputing TV-Violence Link,* Los Angeles Times, June 30, 1983, pt. IV, at 8.

76. *See* Huesmann & Eron, *Cognitive Processes and the Persistence of Aggressive Behavior,* 10 AGGRESSIVE BEHAVIOR 243, 250 (1984), in which the authors present evidence tending to support the violence hypothesis for television in Israeli boys and Polish girls, but tending to support the null hypothesis in Israeli girls and Polish boys.

77. Hoult, *Comic Books and Juvenile Delinquency,* 33 SOC. & SOC. RESEARCH 279 (1948–49).

78. Pfuhl, *Mass Media and Reported Delinquent Behavior: A Negative Case,* in THE SOCIOLOGY OF CRIME AND DELINQUENCY (2d ed. 1970).

79. SEDUCTION OF THE INNOCENT (1954).

80. "Wertham . . . adduces . . . facts and figures which should serve to convince . . . officials that there is indeed such a 'substantial connection' between comic books and juvenile delinquency."*Comic Books and Delinquency,* 91 AMERICA 86 (1954).

81. *See generally,* Spitzer & Hoffman, *A Reply to Consumption Theory, Production Theory and Ideology in the Coase Theorem,* 53 S. CAL. L. REV. 1187 (1980).

82. *See* Thrasher, *The Comics and Delinquency: Cause or Scapegoat,* 23 J. EDUC. SOC. 195 (1949).

83. 50 AM. SOC. REV. 347. 348 (1985).

84. *See generally, id.*

85. I owe a great deal here to the excellent discussion by Krattenmaker & Powe, *supra* note 12, chap. 5, at 1147–56. *See* articles by Eron & Huesmann, cited in note 74, *supra,* for a contrary view.

86. *Id.* at 1156.

87. If one widens the definition to include suicide, the VH-TV loses even more ground. Recent evidence tends to disprove the hypothesized link between television soap opera episodes and subsequent suicides by viewers. Kessler & Stipp, *The Impact of Fictional Television Suicide Stories on U.S. Fatalities: A Replication,* 90 AM. J. SOCIOLOGY 151. *See also* Baron & Reiss, at note 83 *supra.*

88. *See supra* text accompanying note 15.

89. Krattenmaker & Powe, *supra* note 4, at 1156.

90. *See* W. BELSON, *supra* note 59, at 273–76.

91. *See* M. LEFKOWITZ, L. ERON, L. WALDER & L. HUESMANN, GROWING UP TO BE VIOLENT 39–41, 66–67 (1977).

92. *See* Krattenmaker & Powe, *supra* note 4, at 1154–55.

93. *See, e.g.,* H. EYSENCK & D. NIAS, *supra* note 2, chap. 5; R. LIEBERT, S. SPRAFKIN & E. DAVIDSON, *supra* note 2 (all write as though the truth of the VH-TV is now beyond dispute).

94. W. BELSON, *supra* note 59, is a notable exception.

Perceptions of violence can vary with the context in which the violence is shown and with the personality of the viewer. Gunter, *Personality and Perceptions of Harmful and Harmless TV Violence,* 4 PERS. INDIVIDUAL DIFFERENCE 665 (1985). These factors would also need to be addressed by the would-be censor.

95. 378 U.S. 184, 197 (1964).

96. Apparently, the number of children viewing television does not drop below one million until after 1:00 A.M. *See* Pacifica Found. v. FCC, 556 F.2d 9, 14 (D.C. Cir. 1977).

97. I have found no studies of parental control of television diet, per se. However, there are studies of the effects of parents and children watching programs together. *See, e.g.,* Brody & Stoneman, *The Influence of Television Viewing on Family Interactions,* 4 J. FAM. ISSUES 329 (1983); Williams, Smart & Epstein, *Use of Commercial Television in Parent and Child Interaction,* 23 J. BROADCASTING 229 (1979).

98. *See* Krattenmaker and Powe, *supra* note 4, at 1273–75; *See* Fairchild, *Creating, Producing and Evaluating Prosocial TV,* 10 J. ED. TELEVISION 161 (1984) (creating new programming designated to improve race relations).

99. *See* Huesmann, Eron, Klein, Brice & Fischer, *Mitigating the Imitation of Aggressive Behaviors by Changing Children's Attitudes about Media Violence,* 44 J. PERS. & SOC. PSYCH. 889 (1983).

CHAPTER 7

1. 438 U.S. 726 (1978).

2. *Id.* at 748.

3. *See generally* Powe, *Cable and Obscenity,* 24 CATH. L. REV. 719 (1975).

4. 438 U.S. at 765.

5. 438 U.S. at 748–49. This rationale for regulation has been used in the context of regulating commercial and political advertisements. *See* CBS, Inc. v. Democratic Nat'l Comm., 412 U.S. 94 (1973), Banzhaf v. FCC, 405 F.2d 1082 (D.C. Cir. 1969), *cert. denied, sub nom.* Tobacco Inst., Inc. v. FCC, 396 U.S. 842 (1969).

6. Hamling v. U.S., 418   U.S. 87 (1974).

7. 39 U.S.C. § 3010 (1982).

8. 18 U.S.C. § 1461 (1982). *Cf.* U.S. v. Dellopia, 433 F.2d 1252 (1970) (refusing to apply the statute to purely private correspondence, because of privacy interests highlighted in Stanley v. Georgia, 394 U.S. 557 (1969)).

9. FCC v. Pacifica Foundation, 438 U.S. at 749–50.

10. *See* COMICS CODE, *supra* note 49, chap. 6.

11. *E.g.,* 18 U.S.C. § 1464 (1982) (proscribing "obscene, indecent, or profane" broadcasts).

12. 438 U.S. at 749.

CONCLUSION

1. *See* P. GREENFIELD, MIND AND MEDIA: THE EFFECTS OF TELEVISION, VIDEO GAMES, AND COMPUTERS 73–94 (1984).

Index